This is a beautiful book. When culture and the current events of the world cause us to lose sight of our souls, Jun's words invite us to journey into the most lost parts of our story. By reading her hidden hurts, I was able to reflect on mine. I was able to find a freedom I not only wanted but needed. Powerful, redemptive, and transformative.

ANJULI PASCHALL
Author of *Stay* and *Awake*

With fierce gentleness, Tasha Jun invites us to journey with her as she weaves her story as a biracial Korean woman alongside the age-old ache to belong. Through gorgeous prose, Jun masterfully reminds us that following the way of Jesus invites us to become more of our God-given selves, not less—and that ultimately it's in honoring the fullness of each of our ethnicities and particularities that we truly come to reflect the goodness and belovedness for which we were created.

AUNDI KOLBER
Therapist and author of *Try Softer* and *Strong like Water*

Tell Me the Dream Again is a beautifully written book about the tensions surrounding reclaiming an identity formed by growing up in both eastern and western worlds. Tasha Jun gives the reader a front-row seat as she describes her pains, joys, and challenges as a biracial woman. Woven throughout the book are scriptural teachings and the rich textures and flavors of her ethnic heritage. Tasha's offering will resonate deeply with other multiethnic readers and provide needed insight for all of us who have friends and loved ones who live in liminal spaces.

VIVIAN MABUNI
Author of *Open Hands, Willing Heart* and host of *Someday Is Here* podcast for AAPI (Asian American Pacific Islander) leaders

The lyrical beauty of Tasha Jun's prose alone makes her a must-read author. But *Tell Me the Dream Again* is so much more than that. It's a vulnerable invitation into Tasha's spiritual and cultural awakening—a raw journey that is captivating to read while simultaneously beckoning readers to examine the complexities and pain points of their own stories. As someone without strong ties to my ancestors, I found that Tasha's memoir stirred in me a longing to learn about my family history, and even more, it stirred deeper compassion for those who feel like they've never truly belonged.

BECKY KEIFE
Author of *The Simple Difference* and *No Better Mom for the Job*

Tasha has painted a masterpiece in *Tell Me the Dream Again*. Her poetic and honest storytelling draws us into the many layers of being mixed-race. As someone who identifies as a mixed-race Asian American Christian, I was able to explore my own multilayered story and identity on these pages. As the world continues to grow in mixed-race population, we all need this book!

DORINA LAZO GILMORE-YOUNG
Author, speaker, and podcaster

Tasha killed me softly with her song in *Tell Me the Dream Again*. This beautifully written book shows the power of truth and the vulnerability of grace. This is a guidebook to embracing who you are and loving all God created you to be. *Tell Me the Dream Again* empowers us who believed we weren't enough to see our uniqueness as our divine contribution to the world.

TANORRIA ASKEW
Author, entrepreneur, and social justice activist

Tell Me the Dream Again eloquently and evocatively explores the universal need to be understood and loved. Leave it to an Asian American woman of mixed heritage to guide us through the gritty questions of belonging between worlds and finding our own voice on the other side. Tasha Jun is a master storyteller, and the words in her book were written for us all.

MICHELLE AMI REYES
Vice president of the Asian American Christian Collaborative and award-winning author of *Becoming All Things*

Tell Me the Dream Again

TELL ME
THE DREAM
AGAIN

Reflections on Family, Ethnicity, and the Sacred Work of Belonging

TASHA
JUN

TYNDALE
MOMENTUM®

A Tyndale nonfiction imprint

Visit Tyndale online at tyndale.com.

Visit Tyndale Momentum online at tyndalemomentum.com.

Visit the author at tashajun.com.

Tyndale, Tyndale's quill logo, *Tyndale Momentum*, and the Tyndale Momentum logo are registered trademarks of Tyndale House Ministries. Tyndale Momentum is a nonfiction imprint of Tyndale House Publishers, Carol Stream, Illinois.

Tell Me the Dream Again: Reflections on Family, Ethnicity, and the Sacred Work of Belonging

Designed by Dean H. Renninger

Edited by Stephanie Rische

Published in association with the literary agency of Embolden Media Group, PO Box 953607, Lake Mary, FL 32795-3607.

For information about special discounts for bulk purchases, please contact Tyndale House Publishers at csresponse@tyndale.com, or call 1-855-277-9400.

Library of Congress Cataloging-in-Publication Data

A catalog record for this book is available from the Library of Congress.

ISBN 978-1-4964-5957-2

Printed in Colombia

29	28	27	26	25	24	23
7	6	5	4	3	2	1

For 엄마 and Dad

Contents

Foreword

New Mexico was home to me from the time I learned to ride a bike down the bend in our road, the heat waves from the desert-baked asphalt heaving breath on my sunbrowned knees with every pedal of my legs. Most of my childhood adventures wound along the watermelon-hued switchbacks carved into the Sandia Mountains.

A place can hold both cherished memories and caustic reminders, and when you reminisce, the clock's years spin back as if cranking the handle of a jack-in-the-box. You brace yourself like an anxious child waiting to see what pops up. You anticipate complicated memories. Growing up as a multiracial Asian American girl was like that. Complicated.

I was raised from girlhood in the Badlands, where the plateaus were as flat as the contours of my face, the same face I was made fun of for. "Did you run into a door?

Why is your face like that? Can you even see when you smile, ching-chong?" the kids asked on the playground after pulling their eyes into violent, angry slits.

At night I pulled open the medicine cabinet doors around me and looked at my profile reflected in the folded mirrors. My cheekbones sat high and wide, and I pressed my palms flat against my forehead and nose and mouth. I opened my eyes as wide as they'd go.

I learned that by the slant of my lids and the curves of my face, I was somehow "other." It wasn't until I was in third grade and the bullying intensified that I realized that "other" was synonymous with wrong.

I felt God had somehow made me wrong. I wasn't fully white, and I wasn't fully Asian. Two halves of something that didn't seem to add up to a whole.

"Otherness" is something Asian Americans understand. We're perpetually othered and treated as foreign, even if we are born in America. We're asked where we're really from and what we are. We are congratulated on our English, even if it's our first and only language. We are mistaken for the other Asians because, people joke, we all look alike. Asian women are fetishized, while Asian men are emasculated.

I grew up thinking it was just me who was called "ching-chong China girl" in a singsong voice while kids pulled their eyes into slits. I thought it was just me who could never pull off the eyeshadow tutorials from the images of wide-lidded faces in the glossy magazines.

I thought it was just me who had a well-meaning teacher suggest I do a "Who I Admire Most" speech on Connie Chung because she couldn't think of any other Asian American role models. I was twelve before I read a book with an Asian American character in it, and I gobbled down books with a ravenous hunger for story. There were no shows with Asian American representation. I didn't see reflections of me anywhere I looked. So while other kids dressed up like Michael Jordan, Molly Ringwald, or Madonna, I dutifully donned an oversized boxy blazer, grabbed a bottle of Aqua Net, and shellacked my hair into something resembling a helmet to give my talk on how I became the first person of Asian descent to anchor one of America's major networks and the first woman to co-anchor *CBS Evening News*.

In retrospect, it wasn't that Connie Chung's accomplishments weren't noteworthy. She was a pioneer because so few Asian Americans existed in the public sphere of popular culture, let alone were recognized as part of our history.

One woman, upon hearing my Connie Chung story, replied that it was ridiculous, that diversity was just a way to cause division, because we are all equal in Christ. Her dismissive response was nothing I hadn't heard before or since. Some people refuse to admit that all things are not equitable. Racism, racial profiling, ethnic cleansing, genocide, and the systemic oppression of so many people God created in his image have fertilized the roots of hate and pride and the narrowing of who defines what we exalt and what we justify. The sameness of the stories we tell and the selective mouths they come from stifle us all, leaving the witness to God's church soiled, skewed, or silenced.

We were made for more. Yet we often fail to see that diversity has often meant disparity. But ethnicity was God's initiative, his creative manifesto to paint humanity with vibrancy, color, and timbre. To make each freckle, each speck of color in the iris, to coil hair in wiry locks or lay them smooth like straw, to soak our skin in a thousand colors and paint them over the bodies of his creation. God chose to form languages that click and hum and roll off tongues or rattle in the throat like the whir of a bumblebee, to make words that purr and sing in a prism of different notes.

In recent years, as I began to write publicly, I met other Asian American writers online who gave voice to similar struggles. We connected over common experiences, shared burdens, and kindred revelations. Some of us formed an intimate group of Korean American

Christian women writers and called ourselves the #kimchisisterhood.

When one of us was going through a particularly trying time, the sentiment we all chimed in with was: "Have you eaten?" A very Asian way of expressing love and care is to literally feed one another. A Korean mom will stuff you with love in the shape of dumplings or stews or all manner of steaming bowls. Since we're scattered across the States, our love often arrived through DoorDash or Uber Eats. Nourishing bellies nourishes souls.

When Tasha shared her dreams for this book, I championed her voice and begged for the opportunity to gobble up the pages, because I knew the best books don't just give us a glimpse into someone else's story, they help us reveal our own. I knew her words would be nourishment for my soul, like seaweed soup (miyeok-guk), a healing salve for new growth and flourishing and rebirth. A love song to all of us who haven't always been taught we are fearfully and wonderfully made.

I dog-eared pages and scribbled notes in the margins of her manuscript. But I didn't just see glimpses of myself, of my deep desire for belonging, or the ways our stories mirrored each other. In Tasha's beautiful words, I saw an expansive view of a creative, loving, and merciful God who calls us good and invites us to shalom, to be fully present in our unique identities. A God who made us purposefully, divinely setting us in body and place and ethnicity and culture, for such a time as this. A God who knew that only a body of many different parts would ever be able to reflect his glory.

Alia Joy
Author of Glorious Weakness: Discovering God in All We Lack

Prologue

You can keep as quiet as you like,
but one of these days
somebody is going to find you.
HARUKI MURAKAMI

When I was in high school, I guarded the front door of my home. I only let a handful of friends past the entryway. A rare few knew the smell of our kitchen, the sound of my mother's voice over the television that called out like an extra family member, and me, in the middle of it all.

One time a friend called on a Saturday morning to see if I was free. He wanted to ride his bike over. I'd already used up a handful of excuses about why he couldn't come to my place in the past, and I couldn't think of any more excuses that particular morning. Backed into my own corner, I said yes and hung up, then panicked.

I checked the fridge first to assess the initial smell. I looked for kimchi and leftovers. I searched the family room for evidence: Did we appear to be normal? The low table we gathered around to eat at while watching TV suddenly seemed way too conspicuous. Asian crackers in a small bowl sat on top of the table. The bright pink heated floor pad sprawled beside it. All the things that were familiar and normal to me stared back as if we were in a face-off.

Whose normal would win: mine or my friend's? Whose normal was worthy enough? What I didn't have words for then was a need to show up, not normal enough, but white enough.

When I answered the door a few minutes later, I told my friend something had come up and I had to go. We talked for a bit on the doorstep. I was wearing a hoodie and stretching the sleeves over my fisted hands again and again as we talked. He frowned while I fumbled through explanations that didn't make sense even to me until he finally gave up, then turned and rode away.

This wasn't a monumental moment but one of many little moments like it throughout my life. Thinking back on it now, what stands out to me most is the way I blocked the doorway of my house as if there were a wild animal inside. If I close my eyes, I can still feel how tense my body was, how intent I was on not letting that animal out.

I'd come to believe the narrative that my ethnicity and cultural details would turn people away. I blocked the doorway to our suburban home, but the monster that would be discovered was *me*.

I thought I could separate me from me. No one in my family or my inner circles explicitly taught me this narrative of normalcy or told me that my ethnic and cultural identity should be a source of shame. From as far back as I can remember, my family encouraged me to embrace my biracial ethnic identity. Still, the message was everywhere, baked into everything from a lack of representation to an absence of historical education about people who looked and ate and lived like my family did. It was there when classmates pulled at the corners of their eyes on the monkey bars in fifth grade or turned up their noses when I opened my lunch box in the school cafeteria.

At a young age, I learned to believe my Korean normal was embarrassing—a barrier to belonging and an enemy of my deepest longings.

But I didn't fit in when I was in Korea, either. When I went there for the first time to visit my mom's family, she spent a lot of time explaining that I was her daughter as I stood next to her in a store without my dad nearby.

I was stuck in this misfit middle place and had nowhere to go. And no one seemed to care how deeply this plagued me.

There's only so far we can grow in a relationship when we hide large parts of ourselves. There's only so long we can pretend to be color-blind and hide the evidence of our God-given colors. There's only so long we can offer just the front porch or entryway and fool ourselves into thinking this is the way we'll be accepted, the only way we'll be able to have genuine, meaningful relationships. With each new excuse for pushing someone away, we lock ourselves further into isolation.

The lie of cultural assimilation is that it leads to belonging.

———◆———

For most of my life, I struggled to understand and accept who I am. And for many years, I thought my struggle was an individual one—and all my fault, because of something impossibly wrong with me.

I was wrong. This is my story of journeying from childhood curiosity to turmoil and rejection to embrace—and finally back to a redeemed, holy curiosity about my ethnic and cultural identity. This is the story of Jesus' pursuit of all of me, in each of these stages, and how his perfect love convinced me that I am worth being made whole, worth being seen and known, and worth what it takes to live wholly loved and proud of the scent of kimchi—not only in my fridge but on my fingers and permeating the breath I breathe and the words I speak.

I've always been caught between worlds. Ready and not ready, English and Korean, light and dark, weak but prophesied strong, caught between the grief over things lost and the joy over things found. I wandered between these seemingly opposing worlds, struggling to find a voice to speak and a firm place for my feet to land.

There was only so long I could offer Jesus the outer rooms of my heart and pretend that's all there was to me. There was only so long I could fool myself by telling him that he could have everything while I was unwilling to embrace my everything. There was only so long I could keep trying to discard parts that God knit together in me—whether because those parts reminded me of pain or shame, or because those parts seemed to stand in the way of my belonging and my deepest longings. Finally, he called my bluff.

I don't know your story, but you and your details matter too. May my stories help you to bravely and patiently look at your own and lead you back to who you were divinely knit together to be. May it help you see that your identity in Christ is tightly woven with the unique colors, scents, and cultural stories he's given you. May you begin to see the way God's perfect love and Kingdom are reflected in all our diverse experiences and table settings. May you come to know Christ's love for you in every deep part of your heart, mind, body, and soul.

I was blind, but now I see: wild animals are created to be free.

CHAPTER 1

DREAMS AND TIGERS

Once upon a time
when tigers smoked pipes . .

How do I begin to tell one story
when one story begins with two?

She squeezed the word out of her lips, her bright white teeth playing peekaboo: "Ho-raaang-eee."

I'd asked my mother the Korean word for "tiger" after her story was done, moving my mouth to make the same shapes her mouth did, trying to catch the earthy, invisible sounds falling out of it.

As a child, I did everything I could to imitate my mother. I used to study her slender, brown hands, comparing them with mine. I liked to point at the tiny freckle below my right thumb and then at her darker freckle in the same spot—a sign that I could become like her. I learned to laugh loudly, the way she does: mouth wide, eyes watering, and hand fanning our faces as if joy is a fire that can be tamed.

Outside of a few words and phrases, we didn't speak Korean to one another when I was young. However, the language has always pulled at me like a map that promises to show the way home. I can pick it out on a busy city street. I know the curves and movements of its sound. I'm convinced it rests deep within me, asleep and tangled in the beating muscle fibers of my heart.

It was there in my earliest moments, pressing into my bones and ligaments, speaking straight through my mother's thoughts, mouth, and body, helping form my innermost parts. It was the language she used when she fed me and comforted me, when she was affectionate with me, and when she was most angry with me.

It was the language of her womb, my first home.

In college I enrolled in a beginner's Korean course. I showed up for class and burst through the doors with my head high. The four other students in the class were huddled together, their desks pulled into a misshapen circle, talking and laughing in Korean. They were already fluent.

I'd hoped learning the language would bring me closer to home, but instead, I sat in that class for a week, mute and foreign, wondering why I'd been so audacious as to think that I could learn my mother's tongue. The other students would get their easy credit, and I would give up on trying.

I dropped the class.

When I called my mom and told her about it, she was apologetic at first. "Aigoo," she said, trying to simultaneously comfort and patronize me, "I should have taught you more when you little." She kept going, like a song reaching its crescendo. "But you so stubborn! Even when you baby! You don't listen and don't want me to speak Korean. You only speak English. Just like the peas I feed you when you baby—you spit it all back out."

Finally, she reminded me that going to Korean school like other Korean kids would have been hard for me. "You different than other Korean kids. Other Korean kids already know how to speak and have both Korean mommy and daddy to talk to at home. You only have me, and you so soft, and we move all the time."

I remember the year I covered the wall of my room with teen *Bop* magazine pictures. My mom would come in, shaking her head, making comments about how American I was. I would overhear her telling my dad how she regretted not teaching me Korean and how she wanted to enroll me in Korean school. But then she'd argue with herself while my dad listened. She knew the weight of bloodlines and the names thrown at kids like my sister and me, and she knew she wouldn't be able to shield us from those things. She didn't know that even if we didn't go to Korean school, those things would reach for us through geography and generations.

For a long stretch of years, moving kept us busy enough. After I was born, we moved to Wisconsin, then to New York, then to Japan, then back to Santa Barbara, and then to Indiana. Conversations around our dinner table were always about the next place we were headed and the things we'd need to do to get ready to move there. Boxes, missing toys, new streets, and new ways of doing things—all of this was the norm for us.

People and places were always slipping through my little hands, just like Korean words. With each new setting, I regularly checked to see if the freckle I was born with had stayed put.

———◆———

"Tell me the dream again, Mom. What happened to the tiger?" I studied her features, admiring her high, rounded cheekbones and the way her black hair framed the edges of her face, falling stiff and sharp at her collarbone, like the ends of a bristle hairbrush. She sighed at my curious insistence.

"It was night in my dream. Stars everywhere. I watch them, then one kept getting bigger. The light of that star got brighter and brighter. As it grew, it started to turn into a tiger. The white light changed to tiger colors, then I could see the tiger's face. It opened its mouth and roared. It was so loud! My heart was shaking. Then I looked at its face, and it was you. Tiger was you."

I hung on to every word, my heart lifting to the top of my chest. My face held as steady as a poker player, hoping against all odds that the hand I'd been dealt in dreams could actually play out.

"Ho-raaang-eeeee," I said. "Is that right?"

To this day, she has a way of letting me know that I don't say it quite right. It's a sigh, a giggle, or an eye roll, or maybe she repeats it back to me—all to remind me of the chasm of misunderstanding between us. How can there be such stark separation from the one whose body birthed my own? And what are the ripple effects of this kind of dismembering?

I once read that a tiger's roar is so loud it can be heard up to two miles away, that its roar is twenty-five times louder than the average lawn mower.

But for most of my life, I've felt nothing like a tiger.

My voice got stuck somewhere between the plastic walls of an incubator in a California hospital room.

After telling the tiger story, my mom would lift her hands to show me how small I was when I was born. Her eyes bulging, she declared, as if it were the first time she'd told me, "You almost didn't make it! Did you know, you didn't even cry? I'd never seen a baby like you!"

My body hesitated at birth; it wasn't ready. To this day, my mom refers to that first hesitation as the reason I respond slowly to most things.

As I was wrapped up in her tiny womb, the God of the universe formed my limbs, shaped my eyes, and decided to give me my mother's thick, dark hair. Her songs and cries were the first I heard. It was the preferences of her taste buds that were passed down to me.

Her body couldn't keep me as long as it was supposed to. Her water broke at Knott's Berry Farm while my sister and Dad rode a roller coaster and she waited for them on a nearby bench, hands on her rounded belly.

I was forced into the world three months before my due date, ready or not. My lungs weren't finished developing, and upon arrival, I couldn't breathe. Six months of maternal words and songs weren't enough to break my silence. The doctors rushed me in a helicopter from a small Goleta hospital to Santa Barbara Cottage Hospital. No one knew whether life would be too much of a burden for my frail lungs or whether, by a whisper and a prayer, I would come through.

I entered the world without a voice. Somewhere, someone announced, "It's a girl!" But I couldn't respond to their welcome.

For the first twenty-one days of my life, I lived in an incubator. Wires intruded on my isolation while connecting me to a possible future outside the hospital walls. Though I couldn't be fully embraced, fingers and voices reached for me through holes. Prayers spoken to Hananim hung over my compact frame like a blanket.

After I was born, my mom said she felt stronger than she ever had. My dad provided evidence of her words on the pages of a bright pink seventies-era baby book. The cover featured a pale, cream-colored, cloth-diaper-clad baby with blonde, wispy hair and sky-blue eyes. In the margins, he jotted down details in pencil about how my mom and I were doing. He wrote that a few days into my mom's recovery, she felt "ready to fight for [me] to live in any and every way she can."

As a child, I stared at the baby on the front along with the pictures of me taped on the pages. I was half the size of the baby on the cover, and I thought my tiny preemie body with dark hair looked like an alien.

When my parents were finally able to bring me home, my mom fed me and fed me. She poured all her worry about my survival into baby bottles and then into spoons and rice bowls. By the time I was a year old, strangers would stop her as she carried me or pushed me in a stroller to comment on how chubby I was. She fed me until I resembled an Asian version of that blonde baby on the book cover, and more.

In Korean culture, tigers are symbols of strength and power. They are everywhere, from paintings to sculptures that guard tombs. Many Koreans even believe that the geographic outline of the Korean peninsula mimics the shape of a tiger lying down. Years ago, some Korean folktales began with "when tigers smoked," the way Western folktales might begin with "once upon a time." According to legend, there was a time when tigers not only roamed the mountainous land of Korea but also walked around smoking pipes like Gandalf the Grey.

The beloved tiger, the national animal of my mother's homeland, is now extinct in Korea. But the stories live on, and every now and then someone claims to see one, whether in the mountains or somewhere in their dreams. I am the least likely to carry my own tiger story—I've always felt unfit as a Korean but somehow too Korean everywhere else.

The horangi, tiger, from my mother's dreams has lived in my thoughts, silently roaming the backdrop of my imagination, for most of my life. At some point, this tiger who became a girl among the stars went from a recurring dream to a story I clung to. I've kept this story tucked away like a treasure—a treasure I've come back to again and again throughout my life—a treasure I wanted to understand but was afraid of.

◆

We often search everywhere else to find the story we're looking for. But the story we're born looking for is our own. It's the one pressed into our broken bodies at birth, strung among our thoughts and brain waves. It's the one that dances to the beat of our hearts, imprinted with our mother's and father's dreams and given to us with power and loving intention. It's this very story— our own story connected to those of our mothers and fathers, and their mothers and fathers before them— through which Jesus pursues us and is with us.

We're all born with curiosity and a longing to know who we are, because this knowing is inseparable from knowing God. When I walk through an art museum, stare at a painting or a sculpture, and read the small description beside it, I'm moved to learn how the work of art speaks of the person who made it. It carries a message from the heart of the artist. To ignore the details of the piece is to miss the power of its voice. Each work of art drips with purpose and reflection, echoing the time in which it was made and the one who made it. Every color, shape, drip, expression, shadow, and medium was chosen intentionally.

In the same way, we are created beings, lovingly brought to life by our Creator. When we explore the facets and details of our design, the pages of our stories, and the palette of people and places we've come from, we find the purpose and loving intention of our Creator God. We've been birthed into the world with a collection of unfinished stories painted in brushstrokes alongside organs and skin.

My husband and I ordered one of those DNA testing kits a few years ago. We were both excited to spit into our little plastic containers and ship them off to find out more information about who we are. I thought about all the questions I've had stored inside since I was a kid—the ones I incessantly asked my parents, the ones I wrote in messy cursive across my journal pages, the ones tossed around in my mind like wet clothes turning in a dryer without heat.

We filled out our family trees, sending text messages and emails to our families to check names and make sure we got things right as we built one branch after another. Each person added new hints to work through, and each hint led to new discoveries.

On my dad's side, I could go back in time, looking at names and documents from generations and generations before me. From Dutch immigrant farmers who signed their names at Ellis Island to Canadian immigrants to British pastors to ancestors from a specific area of Ireland, I followed the tree lines that reach back into the Netherlands and Great Britain and keep branching through time and generations.

I googled the cities where my ancestors lived, trying to imagine what life was like for them and what they woke up to every day. Countless pictures of villages in England, Ireland, and the Netherlands popped up on my screen. I couldn't get enough of looking at the images or saying the names out loud, trying to pronounce them while imagining the lives of my great-great-grandparents.

On my mom's side, I can go back only as far as her parents. My family tree looks like a one-winged butterfly. There are no hints or leads to filter through. There are only invisible questions. I have dreams and stories, tiny clues in my taste buds, and my dark hair and eyes. Whenever I ignore those clues that speak through every mirror, whenever I dismiss every craving in my mind and stomach, it feels like a personal rejection.

The lack of information on my mother's side— the inability to connect the genealogical dots—tells unnamed stories of injustice, wrongdoing, and oppression. There's an invisible enemy that's always been trying to kill my Koreanness, even before I existed. There's a war against my cultural being, and it's been raging since long before I was born.

I've been angry with God that I never knew my halmoni and haraboji, my grandmother and grandfather. The grief haunts me.

As a child, I felt sad in ways I couldn't grasp or explain. Now I know the sadness came from my mother's losses—not only her loss of my halmoni, but also the loss of an entire country and place. It sits deep in my bones, like a ghost that comes and goes—one whose existence I have no proof for.

My mom told me about losing her parents, then losing her baby brother to an orphanage, about carrying hot goguma (sweet potatoes) in her clothes to stay warm while walking to school in the winter, about being pulled out of school to care for her younger cousins when it was too much for her aunt. She told me they got so hungry that one day her pet rabbit disappeared. The rice was so scarce, there was often none left for her. She added water to help her tummy feel full when the rice couldn't fill it.

With my own privileged and protected view of the world, I would ask her how her parents died and why she had to stop going to school and why she didn't tell her aunt to keep her little brother.

"My dad disappeared in the war, and my mom died in a fire," she told me. "I stopped going to school to help my aunt take care of her kids and her house. My little brother was too young for her to take care of— there were too many of us. All so hungry."

She would list these responses off, one by one, knowing I couldn't imagine any of these scenarios. I would rub my stomach when she said "so hungry," trying to feel what she felt.

Before I was born, the answers to my questions about my maternal ancestors were taken away, put to death.

I would ask her, "How can it all be gone?"

She said most of her pictures were lost in a house fire when she was a girl. She would recount the few memories she had, but there were so many missing pieces.

Even so, God works in the realm of the impossible. He hears beyond the layers of silence. He makes movement where things have been put to death. If we listen closely, look intently, and stay awhile, we will find ways to rebuild what was removed or silenced.

The stories of our parents and grandparents, of nations and people groups, were never intended to conquer one another. They were meant to be bound together. The world tells us that the only way to evolve is for one story to win while the other story assimilates until it's invisible. The world tells us that we can move on without those stories—that we can let the past be the past, as if there's a clean boundary when it comes to time.

But it was never meant to be that way. Our stories and our very beings are made to reflect the image of God together. The wombs we're born from, like the dust and rib God held and created from, are made to matter to one another. He placed his image in Adam and Eve. He looked into their eyes, male and female, and all who would come from them—like you and me—and saw the fullness of his own reflection.

———◆———

A few years ago, my mom mentioned that she wished we could be together for Chuseok, an important Korean celebration in the fall. It was September, and the kids had just started a new school year. I asked her to tell me about it, and she said it was a holiday where families took time off work to be together. They ate rice cakes, and children bowed to their elders and dressed in traditional hanbok to celebrate the fall harvest.

I peppered her with more questions, and soon I could

tell she was overwhelmed and flustered by the amount of information I was asking for. I knew she wished I just understood, like a Korean daughter should, and yet I had no past experience to look back on.

It's strange to rely on Google and DNA apps to understand who I am and who my ancestors are. When my mom doesn't know how to describe something, I ask the Internet. It's how I learned what I was supposed to do for my mom's hwangap—her sixtieth birthday celebration. It's how I found out that most of the Korean words I know are lullabies, phrases about passing gas, or ways to cuss someone out. It's how I found maps to show my kids where their halmoni is from and how I found more Korean books and resources to learn things I feel I should already know.

And eventually, it's how I learned to start celebrating Chuseok and what this holiday likely meant to my family in generations past.

Last year I drove to the nearest Korean grocery store on a cold October day. I was the only one in the store, aside from the store clerk. I went up and down the aisles, studying each of the products. I found songpyeon and other rice cakes and stared at the packaging, wondering how I was supposed to defrost the one that felt hard as rocks, and I spent five minutes trying to decide which kind of gochugaru I needed for making kimchi.

At the checkout, I placed the big bag of gochugaru, the containers of gochujang and doenjang, rice cakes, frozen pajeon, kongnamul, shrimp crackers, and my favorite Nongshim honey crackers on the counter, but the clerk still spoke to me in English. He looked at the songpyeon and explained that it needed to be steamed from frozen, while the others could be set out to thaw. I decided to say thank you in English even though I knew how to in Korean.

I called my mom on the way home to tell her what I'd found, while chomping through an entire pack of injeolmi, the way I used to as a kid. We talked about how we would plan a belated celebration and mark the holiday together, like Korean families do, when our calendars and school schedules would allow.

I felt a surge of anger that we still had days on our calendar like Columbus Day to honor a man who didn't actually discover anything that wasn't already discovered, while some Americans like us find it nearly impossible to carry on the traditions and celebrations of our heritage.

My mom mentioned that she wanted to set up the table in a certain way, like she'd seen in one of the K-dramas she liked to watch. It hit me that she didn't celebrate Chuseok when she was growing up because she couldn't. Because of the war, her family didn't have enough money for a feast of traditional foods, and there was barely any family left to reconnect and reunite.

My mom was born in the aftermath of a thirty-five-year Japanese colonization, with remnants of that oppression everywhere. And though the occupation officially ended before she was born, the ripple effects could still be felt.

She was five years old when the Korean War began and eight years old when it ended. For almost the first decade of her life, both her home and her family were in a constant cycle of disaster, restoration, survival, and trauma.

Her earliest memories were made in the shadow of war: leaving on foot for a safer city in the south that took days to get to, bringing food to her dad in a dirt bunker, seeing dead bodies on the streets, and not having enough food to eat. So while she knew about the holidays, she had very few memories of celebrating any of them.

Only now, as a halmoni herself living in Arkansas, nine hours away from her daughters, sons-in-law, and grandchildren, was she trying to piece it all back together with the help of K-dramas and Korean social media outlets.

After hanging up, I cried the rest of the way home, realizing my mom was rebuilding her own

Koreanness—piecing the lost things back together, bit by bit. These celebrations had been stripped from her during postwar times, and her lonely immigration to the US took whatever shadow remained of these traditions even further away. If she wanted to mark these celebrations, she didn't always have the language or the grocery stores to find what she needed, let alone the energy after eking out a living in a world where she didn't fully belong. For the first time, I realized she felt like all she had to pass on to my sister and me was scraps.

But those scraps—the same ones I often questioned or was embarrassed by, the ones that seemed easily tossed aside—are everything now.

CHAPTER 2

MOTHERS AND FATHERS

All our roots go deep down,
even if they're tangled.

NAOMI SHIHAB NYE

We sat in a circle, and I clutched a notebook on my lap to record our prayer requests. We took turns, one woman after another sharing about their kids, their worries, their friends and family, decisions that needed to be made. I wrote down each request, until the last woman asked for prayer about the rising racial tensions in our nation.

It was 2014, and I was a young mom with a baby and a toddler, coleading a group of fellow suburban moms at the large church our family attended. A few months earlier, eighteen-year-old Michael Brown had been fatally shot by a police officer in a suburb of St. Louis. The suburb, Ferguson, became a name on the tip of our nation's tongue.

The varied reactions and the silence around our circle shifted something in the group when the topic turned to current events. One woman responded quickly, saying how hard it must be to be a police officer, while bypassing the tragedy of a lost life. I sat there mute, wanting to speak up but not sure where to begin. One minute we were sympathizing with one another over toddler woes and the next I suddenly felt like we might be living on different planets. However invisible and practically ignorable the shift was initially, it shed light on us—that illuminated the distance between some of our life experiences and perspectives.

A few weeks later, I was sharing a bit of my own personal story surrounding race and identity with this same small group. I'd never told these friends about this part of my life before, but I wondered if relating some of my experiences would help them understand how close to home the national headlines actually were, even as we were seemingly insulated in our suburban lives.

I told the women what it was like for me to move to Indiana from California as a teenager and the things that were said to me as one of the few Asian Americans in the school. I told them how often I thought about my own children as they grew up and faced similar issues and new ones too.

As we gathered our things to leave, one of the women turned to me and said, "I don't even think of you as Asian!" She said it with a smile, offering it as a compliment or as something to ease the discomfort she must have assumed I felt, being the only Asian in the room.

I stared at her, with images flashing through my mind of my mom singing to me in Korean or feeding me a rice ball wrapped in lettuce with a dollop of ssamjang, then awkwardly mumbled, "Well, I am very Asian."

Early on in my walk with Jesus, I was taught that being made new in Christ and having my identity rooted in him meant I could start fresh—I could be whoever I wanted to be. I could hide behind that explanation of identity and never worry about where I came from or the unmistakable scent of my Koreanness. I could roll my eyes when I had to check a race box I didn't fit into anyway and pretend it didn't matter anymore. I could be excused from having my ethnicity play any significant role in my life and my relationships. I could discard my heritage and assimilate and finally become comfortable enough to belong to the ranks of normal.

But even as I said those things and professed to believe them, I still hid. I still felt impossibly alone. The cultural Christianity I'd come to know said I could leave my cultural identity at home and sever my Koreanness in exchange for a new family that would welcome me—and it was all for the sake of the gospel somehow.

I left the women's group that morning and sat in my minivan with my young kids, handing them snacks from the driver's seat while the engine idled. We watched one minivan after another fill up with moms, kids, and strollers, and drive off until all the cars around us were gone.

The loneliness crept over me until it felt consuming. Instead of running from it like I had in the past, I let it sink in, right there in the church parking lot, while I listened to the *crunch, crunch* of Goldfish, in between my toddler son's retelling of the Old Testament stories he heard in class that day.

I knew these women, their children, their worries, their fears. But did they know me? I could talk to them about our birth stories and listen to them share about their childhood and their parents. I saw the way breakfast casseroles and church potlucks came naturally to them, perhaps like their mothers before them. While they responded to group icebreakers with ease, I was in a state of internal panic over how much explaining I would need to do about my Koreanness so my honest response would make sense.

One time we were supposed to find an object on us or in our purse that we could use to describe ourselves. I opened mine and found a colorful cloth face mask that my mom had sent me. (This was years before the pandemic brought face masks into the mainstream.) I immediately knew no one would understand and pushed it under my wallet. I didn't want to be a culture teacher or offer something about Asian culture for everyone to laugh at in my attempt to explain a normal part of my life and relationship with my mom. I don't remember what item I ended up choosing, but I'm pretty sure it didn't mean much to me.

Now I knew I could be there among them, leading, laughing, listening, and still allow myself to be unseen. For the sake of some false sense of unity, we could refrain from discussing politics, current events, and whether we'd vaccinated our kids, but that didn't mean those topics weren't under the surface. Was this the selfless laying down that was required of me for the sake of community and unity? Was this the burden that everyone was expected to carry, or were only the women of color expected to do that?

And what about the echoes of my mother and father? What about my first taste buds—not the ones I acquired to attend, belong, pitch in, and survive in places like this? Would these friends I loved ever see in me the land where tigers once smoked pipes? Or was that too much to ask of those I called friends?

In the following months, the more I brought up recent news events or talked about the Black Lives Matter movement or shared a little more about my own story, the more alienated I felt. I had chosen not to share those things in the past, but I couldn't hold them in any longer.

As I read the news and watched what was happening in the world, it was as if those things reached for me and peeled back my own layers of self-protection and self-preservation. Simultaneously, as a new mom, I couldn't help but feel a growing urgency as I looked into my young son's eyes, wondering what kind of world my children would grow up in.

I also knew that if I didn't take the risk of sharing honestly what was on my heart, I would never be able to fully belong in a place that had become dear to me. I brought these things up not to stir the pot or ruffle feathers but because I couldn't pretend or ignore them any longer. I knew it wasn't my responsibility to give others an easier, more familiar version of myself to love. Still, it wasn't easy to move away from the expectation of presenting myself as colorless to appease a theology of color blindness that permeated so many of the spaces I found myself in. The more I risked opening up, the more I saw this mindset everywhere, lodged in people I loved, like a barrier between us.

Color-blind theology has always been a sugarcoated death threat to everything Korean in me. It pretends to offer something sweet, but it does so at the expense of deep connection and community. At first glance, the claim of not seeing color sounds nice—like a promising answer to division and hatred. While it might stem from a desire for unity, it creates only a false unity that requires some to erase their colors while others have little at stake.

True unity requires whole people, full of their colors—and hard, holy, humbling work.

◆

When my dad brought my mom home to meet his parents for the first time, my mom said Grandpa Dallas stared at her without speaking for at least thirty minutes.

"Yeah, his eyes were this big," she told me, stretching her eyelids as wide as they would go. "He'd never had an Asian person like me in the house before!" She pointed at herself, chuckling as if she'd just told a joke.

Grandma Margie stared too, but she was friendly. She immediately hugged my mom in a pillow-like embrace, then pulled her into the kitchen, where a potato chip–covered casserole browned in the oven. My mom had never had a potato chip casserole before.

My dad says he doesn't remember the details of that first meeting, but he confirmed that he himself had never seen an Asian person until after high school graduation, when he met a Chinese American man while working in his dad's store. It was the late sixties, and soon after that he would join the navy, go to boot camp, then fly to the Philippines and board his first naval ship, the *Guadalupe*. He met my mom when he was back on US soil, when she waited on him at a restaurant.

I loved listening to my parents tell stories of their friendship and how that friendship led to trust and eventually to a proposal at the foot of Serra Cross, La Loma de la Cruz, with the city of Ventura ahead and the Pacific Ocean behind. My mom likes to tell my sister and me how many times she cut and dyed her own hair during that time and how my typically calm and steady dad responded with shock and surprise. Once she cut pixie-short bangs; another time she dyed her hair orange to match her burnt-orange Volkswagen bug. They told us how my dad used to scuba dive and bring her lobsters and sea urchins. They'd go hiking and have picnics, and I sensed their world was simple and kind then, like a window when time stopped in between their completely incompatible pasts, promising them the future.

My dad grew up in Fillmore, a small town in California that sits at the foot of the Topatopa Mountains. He grew up surrounded by Spanish-named streets and the scent of oranges. I used to search his old yearbooks to see if I could find any Asian faces among the rows of black-and-white photos. I wanted to prove him wrong and find the one Asian who was there all along.

I stared at my dad's subtle smile in tenth grade, fascinated by the fact that the dad in these pictures had never seen a person like my mom or imagined someone like my sister or me yet. I envisioned him waking before dawn to deliver milk jugs to front porches alongside the migrant workers who worked the earth in that small valley town, and I wondered what my mom was doing in those same moments, miles and time zones away.

Later I would sit at that table where my mom ate her first potato chip–covered casserole, chatting with my grandparents while staying with them for a couple of weeks over the summer. We listened to Paul Harvey telling stories on their scratchy radio after my grandpa read a page from the *Our Daily Bread* booklet. I kept an eye on my Grandma Margie's metal tin on top of the fridge as an incentive to get through dinner. She kept homemade oatmeal cookies in that tin.

I shoveled the skinny, long-grain rice into my mouth,

surprised by each flakey forkful flavored with cinnamon and butter instead of the stickiness and hints of kimchi juice that traveled across my dinner plate back home. I wondered what was wrong with the rice while trying to imagine my grandpa silently staring at my mom for so long. Did he see my mom's face in my own now? Did he see his son's smile hiding under my cheekbones?

———————◆———————

Only about fifty years ago, the country I was born in had laws in place to prevent my birth. Laws with righteous-sounding titles like the Racial Integrity Act had formalized and normalized racism in the United States of America, and up until 1967, sixteen states still had anti-miscegenation laws.

Like the Nuremberg Laws from Nazi Germany, which were intended to "protect German blood and honor" and led to the Holocaust itself, anti-miscegenation laws restricted interracial marriage and enforced racial segregation in public places. Some of the same ideology and blatant racism were written into the American laws to "protect whiteness."

It wasn't until June of 1967, with the verdict of Loving v. Virginia, that the Supreme Court ruled all laws prohibiting interracial marriage to be unconstitutional. My parents were married in 1975 in California.

While such a union had been legal in California since 1948, it's hard for me to comprehend that in many states, less than a decade prior, in my grandparents' and great-grandparents' America, my parents' marriage would have been illegal.

Two inanimate objects tie me to my great-grandma Carrie, my grandpa's mother. One is a picture of her holding me in her arms on my first birthday. My cheeks are stretched open like a balloon that's been blown up to the point of popping, and my mouth is framed with white icing and yellow cake crumbs. The rest of my face is strawberry red from crying. Great-grandma Carrie is smiling wide and wearing a white sweater that matches her short curls. She's holding me up while my mom stands on the other side of me, patting my back for comfort.

The second object is her cast-iron pan. Whenever I use it, I think about how she made cornmeal mush and pancakes fried in bacon grease for my grandpa and his siblings on their Nebraska homestead. In a manuscript he wrote about his life, my grandpa described the wind blowing so violently in the small town of Story that they had to go into their outdoor cellar until the tantrum subsided. There were no trees to soothe and slow the storm as it unleashed its anger over their house.

I tried to imagine being a mother who had to hide her kids underground, leaving everything in the house, like that cast-iron pan, with no guarantee those belongings would remain a few minutes later. Did she ever imagine how her family would survive and grow, and that someday she'd have a great-granddaughter who would still use that pan, frying and burning kimchi-jeon, Korean pancakes, on its black surface?

On a road trip fourteen years ago, my family and I stopped at a rest area in Nebraska. My husband and I were on staff with Cru, driving to a national staff conference in Colorado. We were brand-new parents, with our six-month-old firstborn in tow. We didn't have any reason to be in Nebraska other than to get through it.

I sat on a concrete bench to feed my son, mesmerized by the way the wind sang through the plains surrounding me. I felt a connection to the prairie grass that bent and bowed to an unseen power—a power that could both tickle my nose and wreak havoc through an entire neighborhood. At the same time, I felt out of place, noticing that everywhere we stopped throughout the state, there was no one who looked like my son or me. I tried to imagine my grandpa growing up there and my great-grandma being a new mom like I was, sitting on that bench.

Being biracial is being tied to places, people, and a history that wouldn't have welcomed me. It's forging a new way forward with my body, trying to hold all the collisions within the tiny beating space under my ribs. It's learning to hold more than one white flag and to mediate the broken places between nations and races while I choose what's for dinner on a Wednesday night. It's finding the parts of my history that wouldn't have accepted me, the parts that held power, and the parts that were hidden and pushed down—and then giving voice to the rest of the story.

For me as a mom, it means passing on to my kids the rice bowls my mom passed on to me. It's seeing the Asianness in my kids and affirming it in a world that affirms only their whiteness or sees assimilation as a nonnegotiable. It's finding my voice in a world that questions or ignores their Asianness while denying that it's doing so, a world that asks them just how foreign they are and tempts them to settle for being seen through the lens of shame or entertainment.

At a Thanksgiving gathering just months before Grandpa Dallas died, I sat on the floor beside him while he sat in a velvety brown armchair. He'd become quieter in the days and weeks since my grandma's Alzheimer's disease had progressed. My mom and aunts were in the kitchen, and my dad and uncles were on the other side of the living room, arguing about politics. I kept looking at my grandpa, wondering what he thought of the younger men, arguing like they knew everything.

I wondered if he thought I should be in the kitchen with the other women.

I asked him what he was thinking. He turned to me and said, "Keep writing. You are going to be like Moses someday, making a new way. I just know it."

Between the two groups of our family, with one arguing and the other clanking pots and pans, it felt like we were the only two people in the house.

———◆———

In the rare moments when my mom sat down to play or rest with me when I was growing up, she turned child-like. One afternoon after school while living in Tokyo, we watched cartoons, and I brushed her hair as if I were the mom and she were the daughter. When she brushed my hair, I got teary from the pull of tangles, but when I brushed hers, her tears fell from the grief over not having someone to brush her little-girl tangles away.

She told me how she would do anything to have her mom brush her hair. She said if she could go back, she'd never complain about how her mom told her what to do. She said all she remembers is complaining, and then her mom was gone.

"What do you mean, she was gone?" I asked her.

She shook her head and said I wouldn't understand.

She sat on the floor and cried for her mother while

I sat silent on the couch behind her, towering over her bent, shaking shoulders. My knobby eight-year-old knees framed the back of her black head, and I felt a stab deep under my rib cage: both of us grieving the years of having no mother or halmoni to brush our hair.

Grief passes through generations. It swims through oceans, and it scales borders. It can be felt through a little girl's hairbrush and imagined in the margins of the incomplete stories our mothers and fathers tell us. We feel the weight of dead dreams and empty pages, no matter our age or language.

Sometimes I strive to imagine my halmoni's and haraboji's faces, believing for a moment that if I think hard enough, they'll appear. But they never do. I've started naming the things I never knew but lost: their faces, their voices, their love, what made them laugh, the way they might have fed me, scolded me, or held my hands in theirs. I say it all out loud or scribble it, barely legible, in my journal.

My body feels these losses, and I am as fragile as a teacup on the edge of a table that my kids run around and around in a game of tag, oblivious, until it falls off the edge and shatters.

When I stayed with my paternal grandparents, I adjusted to their structured lives. It was comforting to me, a kid who had moved more times than she could count on one hand and who was trying to figure out how to build cultural bridges by the time she was in the first grade without even knowing it. Boring days in their quiet house on Halcyon Road gave my tiny body room to breathe, daydream, tie stories together in my mind, and just be.

They woke up at five thirty every morning, and most mornings that I stayed with them, I woke up while it was still dark because something in the Central Coast California air irritated my lungs. By morning, every breath whistled, and I would stand upright to see if that would help the air get in. I once walked across the hall to peek into their room while they slept, hoping I wouldn't cough. The clock stared at me with its oversize red digits; it was also wide awake.

As I stepped into the kitchen, the linoleum tiles with tiny flowers creaked. I thought about the cookies on top of the fridge and considered whether I could sneak one out and eat it before their alarm went off. I decided not to and stopped to look at the painting on the wall. I can't remember if it was my great-aunt Violet or my great-grandma Carrie who painted it. The scene depicted a field with a small stream running across it. I reached for the picture, wanting to feel the thick dried paint under my fingertips.

Something about the painting pulled at my insides. I wanted to see around the corner, where it looked like the stream came rushing from. Even then, as a little girl, I was homesick for something more than any home I'd ever known. I wanted to belong to these places I'd never been to before—the ones that wouldn't have had a little Asian girl in them.

I scurried back into the warmth of the guest room bed. Once my grandparents woke up, I listened to them shuffle around in the room next to mine. They used the bathroom, opened and closed drawers, then eventually came out in matching red and blue jumpsuits for their morning walk.

I popped out of bed, got dressed, and found my shoes.

We walked out of the house, then down a couple of short blocks before we were on one of the main streets of Arroyo Grande. We passed the old pink Victorian home that was turned into an inn, and my grandpa stopped and picked a plum from the tree in front of it. He wiped it off on his jumpsuit, then handed it to me with a big smile. As I bit into it, the juice squirted from the sides of my mouth and dripped down my face toward my chin. It was perfect.

My grandparents laughed, delighted to see me enjoying the fruit they offered me.

One afternoon, my grandma sat me down in an orange and brown plaid chair by the front door. She usually brought me along for whatever chore or activity she had planned for the day. Sometimes she sat down to play Uno with me, but mostly she kept her hands busy. I sat in the chair while she knelt beside me and faced me, smiling.

I didn't know where to put my hands. I kept looking from her to the door to the table next to me until she reached into a drawer and pulled out a little booklet. She moved at a slower pace than usual, like she was trying to capture peace from the air and make the room stand still.

She looked at me and asked, "Have your mom and dad ever shared about Jesus with you?"

I rolled through my memories, trying to remember what they'd told me. A random Sunday school memory from a random church we tried somewhere—I didn't remember where, because we'd only gone once—came to mind. We made a butterfly craft. I colored it in blue and purple, then cut it out with scissors that hurt my hand because they were too small. I remembered something on a chalkboard about Jesus making our lives new like butterflies, and how the lesson gave me a fluttery feeling in my chest.

I looked at my grandma. "I think so," I said. "Jesus makes us into butterflies in heaven, right?"

She laughed a little and asked if she could share her little booklet with me, and told me how important it was. She read through the pages, each one with a key point: who God was; who God created; how those he created, like me, had sinned; and how Jesus paid the price for our sins and offered us new life.

She closed the little booklet, then looked up and said, "We all need Jesus. Do you feel that need? Do you want him to come into your life?"

I felt that same fluttery feeling, without understanding everything she'd read to me. I didn't know anything about what a life with Jesus would be like or feel like, but when she asked me if I felt I needed him, I knew the answer was yes.

She invited me onto the floor with her, and we prayed together. I repeated after her, hoping I would still get to be a butterfly someday.

When we had rice at their house, I told them about the rice we had at home—how different it was. My grandma just nodded and chuckled. I was unsure what she thought about our rice. Did she care? When my grandma filled my bath and handed me a fluffy square washcloth, I told her about the long nylon washcloths I was used to and how my mom would scrub my back to reach the places I couldn't.

She walked out and left me alone in the lukewarm water, giggling to herself a little at our Korean bath custom while I wondered who would scrub my back.

I come from a legacy of war and community, of survival songs and scandalous sins and unexpected strength. I come from the mountainous lands of Korea and immigrant homesteads built on stolen prairieland in Nebraska. My body has grown from a million bowls of short-grain, sticky rice and the stories of poverty and loss that stick to my insides—and my kids' insides, just the same.

To see me and know me is to hear me bearing witness to these songs and stories while I share prayer requests and bring something other than a casserole to our church potluck. To come close enough to love me is to be willing to change the script about what's allowed to be normal, and it's being willing to question what systems put and keep normal in place. To know me and love me is to see and welcome my very Asian self in all its uniqueness and complexity, whether that's how I respond during an icebreaker in a church's moms' group or in the way I am wired to lead and listen.

In Jesus' final prayer with the disciples the night

before he was led away to be crucified, he prayed for his followers to be united just as he is united with his Father and the Holy Spirit.[1] It's always felt too other-worldly for me to grasp how distinct but intertwined the Trinity is. But then again, when I think of the way I am irrevocably connected to my mom and dad, to stories that take place in the aftermath of a Korean war and on a homestead in Nebraska, to my grandpa and grandma in Arroyo Grande and my halmoni and har-aboji whose faces I never knew but see in my own, I feel the gravity of Jesus' final prayer pulling my hands and feet to the common earth below.

This ground we stand on has held us from the begin-ning of creation, burying our sins and fractures, shaking us from its molten lava core to wake up to one another, teaching us with the falling leaves every autumn to lament, mending our brokenness with rain and resur-rection every spring, nourishing us with food and glu-ing us back together the way mud sticks and sloshes until the sun warms it back to dust.

The ground where we stand, build, plant, hike, sin, and love is no longer mere dirt but something more like magic. God's very hands hold the nations and worlds together as one family and one story, passed down from grandfathers and grandmothers, halmonis and harabo-jis, mothers and fathers, aunties and uncles, sisters and brothers. These stories come from war-torn Korean streets to central Californian houses with orange trees to reflect the ultimate Creator, the Word who was with God in the beginning[2] and is God throughout the rest of all stories, the Abba Father, the hovering Spirit, and the Lamb of God. And through every one of those stories, God has woven in the thread of the imago Dei, intended to be seen, known, celebrated, and loved.

CHAPTER 3

SHADOWS AND FIG LEAVES

We believe the one who has the power. He is the one who gets to write the story. So when you study history, you must ask yourself, Whose story am I missing? Whose voice was suppressed so that this voice could come forth? Once you have figured that out, you must find that story too. From there you begin to get a clearer, yet still imperfect, picture.

YAA GYASI

We moved from Goleta, a little city just outside of Santa Barbara, to Noblesville, Indiana, at the end of my eighth-grade year. On my first day of school, I wore a white button-up shirt covered in bright yellow, orange, and red flowers. My Californian, mixed-race skin looked caramel brown, and my black hair stood out like a Sharpie on a white page as it fell against my light-colored shirt collar.

I went to the office like I was supposed to, where a boy was waiting with a woman from the office staff.

He told me that he'd always wanted to live in California and become a surfer, and that he would walk me to my homeroom class. We walked down the dark halls lined with green lockers, and when we arrived, the teacher paused midsentence. He beckoned me to stand beside him at the front and introduced me as the new student.

I looked at the class sitting in front of me, suddenly wishing I weren't wearing such bright clothing that highlighted my dark skin and hair. I scanned the faces—there were none like mine. Not one. It was the first time I'd been in a classroom as the only Asian American. It was the first time I'd ever thought about being in a place where I was the only one—the first time I'd thought about being different.

That day I was asked by perfect strangers—fellow students—if I was the new Chinese girl, the new Hawaiian girl, the new Mexican girl. And: "Are you the new girl from California—what are you, anyway?"

For my second day at the new school, I worked frantically to find anything that would hide what stood out in those musty school halls. I ended up wearing the baggiest navy-blue T-shirt I could find and baggy black jeans.

The impulse to try to hide and shrink after being questioned and singled out was a force I'd never felt before. At thirteen, I instinctively knew how to sew my own fig leaves, trying to hide in plain sight.

That year, I went from being an already quiet girl to being as close to mute as possible. I slid through the next four years stoic and stone-faced, taking cues from everyone around me about what parts of me didn't fit, while working hard to hide them. The grief over that ongoing loss was always there, but I didn't know how to name it, and I made sure no one else would know.

———◆———

When Adam and Eve realized they were naked, they became acutely aware of their physical differences, and instead of celebrating God's image in each of them, they felt shame. Their shame pushed them to conceal their differences, and they sewed fig leaves for clothes.[1] This played out the narrative Satan had set forth—that maybe God was holding out on them and didn't have their best interests in mind.

They learned to cover, to hide, to see their differences as a means of separation, oppression, and shame. Suddenly, as a result of their disobedience, there was a hierarchy and a power struggle at work, and what was intended for good, beauty, and celebration was broken. And now, any time we reject a part of ourselves that makes us distinct—including our ethnic and cultural identity—it's all part of this ongoing brokenness.

One day after school, not long after we moved, I grabbed a snack and turned on the TV. I flipped through the channels and eventually landed on a talk show—I can't remember which one—and started doing my homework while it was on in the background. The episode was on racism, and a panel of guests was on stage, fighting and screaming at one another.

Some guests were Black and others were white, and as I stopped to watch, I scribbled a poem in one of my school notebooks. I don't remember the exact words, but it was something about watching people scream with such loud voices while people like me were kept out of the conversation, like a small fish won at a summer festival and put into a jar—all eyes and no voice, waiting to die on someone's kitchen counter.

By thirteen, I'd learned to believe the lie whispered in my ear like the one the sly serpent told Eve and all the daughters after her: that to belong I would have to get rid of everything that kept me from blending in and hide all that colored me in as the full version of myself. I'd already learned to question the way I was made and whether the one who made me had good intentions in mind.

I believed that cultural assimilation would give me

a way to belong and move through life with less shame, but instead of offering me belonging, it only isolated me further. My fig leaves not only separated me from my classmates and from true friendship, but they also distanced me from my family and all the things I knew as home.

◆

When I was a child, my family made three trips to Korea to find and then reconnect with my mom's family. From the moment we set foot in the country, people stared at my sister and me with wide eyes. Strangers mumbled and whispered to each other when we walked by, looking at us, and then at our mom and dad, and then back at us. We were Korean blemishes, evidence of unrequited national love, honyol daughters in the motherland where pure bloodlines are sought after and protected at all costs.

Though I hadn't been born there, I imagined that going to Korea would feel like a homecoming. But when we arrived, we were treated as perpetual strangers. In Korea, the blame for historical hurts and wrongs was placed on our still-growing shoulders.

One summer when I was eight years old, we hustled into our taxi after arriving at the airport. My mom sat in front so she could talk to the driver. I sank into the back seat next to my dad, trying to take in the unfamiliar scents and sounds. I studied the taxi driver's seat with the brown beads and the white covering underneath it. I listened to the driver chomping on a piece of chewing gum and watched the way his lips smacked. I noticed each time he looked at my dad and me in the rearview mirror, and I furrowed my brow, trying to grasp the words he exchanged with my mom.

How can I feel at home and foreign at the same time? I wondered. I looked at my dad next to me, with his curly brown hair and wide green eyes, and then at the Korean man in front of me—the one my mom spoke with effortlessly and who understood her in a way my dad and I didn't—and I realized they couldn't be more different.

One day we walked along Haeundae Beach, known for its urban beachfront lined with vendors. I held a little plastic light-up ball that my parents bought me the night before from a street vendor. I carried it proudly, like a symbol of my connection to other Korean children I saw.

As we walked along the beach that summer day, we observed small food stalls, a fortune-teller, and other people enjoying the sunshine. I heard laughter and sharp-edged words I didn't know coming from behind us. Then I felt something drip down my leg while even more laughter erupted. I wiped the moisture from the back of my calf and tried to comprehend what had happened.

Later my mom and dad explained that we'd been spit on because we were biracial Koreans. My sister scrunched her brow in anger, and my cheeks flushed with embarrassment. I was suddenly aware of something about myself I'd never thought to feel shame about before.

I left the light-up ball in the hotel room the next time we went out.

On my first trip to Korea when I was seven, this time without my sister, my parents and I went to a dinner party with my mom's extended family and their friends. I was sitting in the front room with my cousins and a bunch of kids I didn't know. One of the boys kept pointing at me. He was taller than I was, with smooth black hair cut like a bowl around his head.

When we all went outside to play, he poked me with a toothpick. I stared at him, then at the toothpick, too stunned and confused to understand why he'd do something like that.

After the second time, I tried to tell my cousins with flailing hands what happened, pointing at the boy and then at the spot on my arm. I said the only Korean word I could think of: "Apaeo, apaeo." *Hurts, hurts.*

They didn't understand. Everyone else was laughing, especially the boy with the secret toothpick. I tried to stay away from him, on the other side of the group of kids. My stomach turned when our eyes met.

I went inside to see my parents, but they were drinking and laughing, enjoying the other adults. My mom's smile was wide, her cheeks were flushed, and her eyes were twinkling. I didn't say what was wrong but stood by her quietly, wondering which adults were toothpick boy's parents.

"It's boring for you in here," my mom whispered. "Go back and play with other kids."

I went back outside, and we all stayed there until it was dark. Every chance he got, the boy poked me hard—in the arm, in the back, in the neck, in my thigh—while I listened to the adults inside laughing.

When we left, I was so relieved I immediately fell asleep in the car. I never told my parents. Somehow, even as a first grader, I decided I was to carry the world of my mom's loss, and both the worlds that couldn't welcome me, in my tiny elementary-school body. I wanted to stay in Korea forever, and I also wanted to leave for fear of more round-faced boys who would poke my mixed skin with a dirty toothpick to remind me that I don't belong.

When I think about David's now-famous declaration that he was fearfully and wonderfully made,[2] I can't help but marvel at how audacious it was. The Hebrew word he uses at the end of the verse to describe how "well" he knows it is *meod*, which translates to "vehemently, wholly, speedily."[3]

There's an urgency and fullness to this knowing. Our story as sons of Adam and daughters of Eve isn't just one of knowing God separate from our humanity and our own God-made bodies. God intends for us to know him as we come to know ourselves. Our unique selves are to be studied, seen, uncovered, and sought with urgency. Knowing ourselves without shame is *shalom* in action—life unfolding the way it was meant to, the narrative of the Kingdom of God-come-down. In the midst of this, God's dreams come true, unfolding detail by detail in our mothers' wombs.

When God calls out to Eve and Adam after they've eaten from the tree of the knowledge of good and evil, he asks them, "Where are you?"[4] Even though he knows where they are, what they've done, and what the consequences will be, he seeks them out in their hiding.

He does this again and again. When Cain hides

after murdering his brother, God finds him and asks him where his brother is. When Hagar runs from her oppressive life, he asks her where she's come from and where she's going.[5]

God's love will not let us go on hiding forever. His love finds us, stops for us, and searches for those who have been harmed and those who need healing.

And whenever we come near to someone else in hiding, we imitate Jesus, our Immanuel: the God who comes near.

———◆———

In college I had a creative writing professor who consistently encouraged and challenged me to grow. After one particularly grueling critique session with other student writers in his class, I met with him in his office to talk more about my story. Undergrad aspiring creative writers can be awful, and the arrogance in the room during some of those critique sessions almost made me vomit some afternoons.

Even so, I'll never forget them or how the red marks covering my writing helped me become a better writer. It was the first time I'd offered my inner writing world to people I didn't know and then sat through an hour of their honest feedback.

My creative writing professor's office was dark and

narrow. He sat at his desk, looking at papers, his glasses on the tip of his nose. The sleeves of his gray-striped button-down shirt were rolled up, and he had a red pen in his right hand. He always marked up my stories with red pen.

Across from the desk were bookshelves filled with volumes. Without looking up at me, he asked what I thought about dog-earring book pages. Put on the spot, I waffled, wondering what I thought and what he thought.

"I don't know," I finally said, at a slight notch above a whisper.

He looked up, and I could tell he didn't believe me.

"What do *you* think about them?"

"Never," he said. "I never dog-ear my books." He beckoned me to sit down across from him, and he put the papers he was holding on the desk where I could see them. My story.

We talked about grammar and the critique class, and then after flipping through a few pages, he asked me what I was hiding in my writing. Again, as with the dog-ear question, I waffled, unsure what I was hiding and how to confess it when I couldn't even confess it to myself. I wanted to be an already-good creative writer—someone who knew the right answer without having to make a journey to get there.

My professor would have none of it. He told me to turn around and pull certain books off his shelf. He told me I was doing something he couldn't teach no matter how he tried—writing from the heart—but I would need to find out what I was hiding before it would get any better.

He asked me what Asian American authors I'd read, and there was only one: Amy Tan. My one Asian American author hero. I told him how much *The Joy Luck Club* had moved me and what it had meant to me.

I left that meeting with a stack of books by Asian American and Asian Canadian authors, and after that day, I began to grow and learn more. I read *Obasan* by Joy Kogawa, *Donald Duk* by Frank Chin, and *A Gesture Life* by Chang-rae Lee. I read Maxine Hong Kingston's *The Woman Warrior* and saw glimpses of my own writing style in hers.

These varied stories veered far from the narrative of white supremacy and opened a whole new world of Asian American stories that reminded me of my mother's laugh. They were liberation stories, and I needed them desperately so I could see and tell my own story. These stories were different from mine, but I saw a reflection of myself in them. I looked in their mirrors and saw my fig leaves.

I was so carefully covered, it would take time and many red marks for me to begin to recognize myself.

CHAPTER 4

SEAWEED SOUP

Food is everything we are. It's an extension of
nationalist feeling, ethnic feeling, your personal history,
your province, your region, your tribe, your grandma.
It's inseparable from those from the get-go.

ANTHONY BOURDAIN

She stood at the kitchen stove, leaning on her right leg. Her tiny left foot rested sideways against her right knee, her leg lifted to resemble a triangle. Her back was toward me, bent over a steaming pot. She dipped a burnt-tipped wooden cooking spoon into the pot, tasting the broth every few minutes.

Growing up, I watched her stand at kitchen counters like this in every house we lived in. She ate leftover rice mixed into cold water for breakfast, with an open glass jar of kimchi nearby. She made ice-cold naengmyeon throughout the summer and then made sujebi, soon-dubu, doenjang, and kimchi jjigae in the colder months. She was always making something during the day, and she rarely sat down.

As a girl, I watched her stir, spoon, and slurp. When I was young, I often requested two simple Korean soups: tteokguk filled with chewy rice cakes (my favorite) and muguk filled with sweet radishes. I was reluctant about most of the other dishes, especially the seaweed soup that resembled a bowl of the ocean, with wet rectangles of seaweed that stuck to my spoon and tongue the way it wrapped around my legs in the ocean. There was something claustrophobic about it—a fear that I wouldn't be able to untangle myself from this plant of the sea. And if I couldn't untangle myself, if I lost control, where would this seaweed and the current it swam in end up bringing me?

When my mom stood over these pots of spicy stew and earth-colored broth, I knew she was remembering. Her mind was elsewhere, and memories I didn't know or understand were being stirred up alongside the softening vegetables.

I often turned away her offered spoonful with a scrunched-up nose and an unyielding "No, thanks." I tried to ignore the fact that I was refusing more than a taste of soup. I told myself it was okay if I'd rather eat chicken noodle like the other kids. I told myself it was only a matter of taste and preference, nothing more.

Right after our first son was born, my parents came to visit and help us transition into parenthood. On their last day with us, my mom stood at our stove over a huge pot making seaweed soup. She stood on one leg, as she always did, and I was a child again.

Peeking under the lid of the pot, my mom rambled on at me from the kitchen of our open-layout apartment while I nursed my son on the couch. She told me how important it was for me to eat this particular soup.

"All Korean women eat it after giving birth," she said. "I didn't teach you enough." Then she insisted on having me try some while she walked across the room with a spoonful. She gently shoved it into my mouth while I tried to make sure none of it dripped onto my newborn son's face.

She raised an eyebrow as if to say, "See? You need it. I'm right." She looked at me, waiting for a response.

I nodded, holding my eyes steady so they wouldn't roll into the back of my head, and she returned to the kitchen with the dripping spoon.

She retrieved another spoonful and shoved it into my dad's mouth while he stood next to her. She stirred the pot once more and said to me, "Finish the whole pot when you done feeding."

I was hormonal and tired, and even though I told her I'd eat it once she was gone, I didn't. I took a few tiny spoonfuls and then poured the rest down the kitchen sink. My son watched from his bouncy seat beside me as the liquid flowed down the drain like a disappearing waterfall.

◆

Almost a year later, I was in a bookstore pushing my son around in his stroller while he fisted Cheerios, and I stopped in the international cookbook aisle. I found a beautiful front-facing hardcover Turkish cookbook and then spotted a thin paperback Korean cookbook beside it, as if it were hiding.

I pulled it out and found an inviting picture of noodles with perfectly placed vegetables on the cover. I flipped through a few pages, and then there it was: seaweed soup. I began reading the author's description about the Korean tradition of giving new mothers this special healing soup. For thousands of years, Korean mothers have made miyeokguk for their Korean daughters when they become mothers. When I became a mother, I dumped mine down the drain.

Standing in the busy Barnes & Noble aisle, clutching book pages in my hand to keep them open to the seaweed soup spread, I cried like a baby, right onto the page. I bought the book I'd ruined with my tears—tears that finally fell over all the years of rejection.

From our very beginnings, we are meant to be fed by our mothers. Upon birth, our bodies are still connected by umbilical cords—tangible evidence of God's design for our nourishment. Even after we enter the world and that cord is severed, we're never meant to be severed from the influence of our mothers as they shape our lives and identities outside the womb.

In Genesis 2, we witness the way God provides for and nourishes his created children. He made all kinds of trees to grow out of the ground that gave sustenance and were also aesthetically pleasing to the eye. Verse 16 says not just that God encouraged Adam and Eve to eat; he commanded them to do so. The Hebrew words God used for eating are *akal* and *tokel.* This isn't just a polite offering of food but more like an urging. He says to eat freely (*akal*), and he adds emphasis by repeating the loving command to eat (*tokel*).

When I imagine God urging Adam and Eve to eat, I picture my mom with a spoonful or a chopstick bite, or a ssambap the size of my fist, practically forcing me to open my mouth and receive what she prepared. "Meoggo, meoggo," she would say. "Eat, eat!" This was how my mom showed her love for me.

Somewhere along the way, imagining God feeding

Adam and Eve like my Korean mother fed me healed something in me. God has been trying to tell me how much he loves me through my mom's food ever since I was in her womb, and in my earliest days when she fed me love until my cheeks and limbs were as round and as full as they could be.

———◆———

When my husband and I were first dating, I told him that I liked Asian food but didn't have to eat it all the time. "I eat pizza and cookies too," I assured him.

I look back now and sense the fear in my words. If I let him know just how much I love Asian food, that it's what I want to eat most of the time and what feels like home all the time, would I be too Asian for us to stay together? I would think of things I'd heard from other Asian Americans, like a childhood friend who told me how important it was not to seem "fresh off the boat" or friends who said that no matter how hard they tried to fit in, people would always find out they were "yellow on the inside." I wondered if Matt would bend toward me or if I would have to let that part of myself go, like I was already used to doing.

Matt didn't grow up with fish as part of his family's diet, and when we first met, he told me he didn't eat it. It gave me pause—not the refusal of fish in particular, but the adamancy I thought I heard in the announcement.

But as time went on, I began to see that I was wrong. After meeting my parents and spending time with them, after listening to me share more stories of my upbringing and become louder and looser about what tastes and scents made me who I am, he drew nearer. He didn't have a thing for Asians like I'd heard from guys before. He wasn't exactly adventurous for the sake of adventure; he was willing and open for the purpose of knowing me and learning to love me for who I was, ethnically and culturally.

One night we went for sushi at his insistence. For me, this was a turning point in our relationship. He ordered and tried all kinds of sushi, realizing for the first time that he liked raw fish and that maybe he could eat other kinds of fish. And more important, I saw that he wasn't adamant about it any longer. I sat across from him, partially wishing he hadn't decided he liked the tuna nigiri so much because that meant less for me, and also shocked by his unassuming courage to try something that, for his entire life, he'd been so sure wasn't his thing.

I've often joked that it wouldn't have worked for me to marry someone who didn't eat fish, but in reality, eating fish wasn't really the big deal. It was witnessing the way he was willing to try something new, to move toward the unfamiliar, to approach me and the unknown with humility, tenderness, and bravery. He changed his mind and decided to *become* alongside me.

Matt has loved and pursued the hidden parts of who I am, even when it would have been easier for him to ignore those parts. Even after I gave him a pass by telling him that eating Asian food didn't matter too much to me, he didn't accept it. In doing so, he offered a safe place for those pieces of me to arise at their own pace, for me to risk being seen and known. He was willing to dig with me, even when it meant bumping up against what he was used to, even when it meant hard things would become uncovered for each of us in the process.

We've been married for seventeen years now, and we laugh about how much has changed over time and how many things are a reality now that we never would have expected. We also laugh about how I've become more and more Asian with time. The truth of it is that I've become more and more myself, and one of the most wonderful things about a good, safe marriage is the experience of being loved in the long, unglamorous, often painful, always awkward process of becoming whole.

The cultural palates God has given us aren't accidents. They aren't sidenotes or accessories. God speaks unconditional love directly through the unique tastes, textures, scents, and appearances of the foods of our mothers and fathers. These tastes aren't meant to be fodder for ridicule or rejection, or to be divorced from our identity as his beloved children. They are divine gifts. It wasn't just my mother's culture I was resisting every time I opposed an offered spoonful of soup or pretended I didn't crave Korean food. I was resisting God's loving intention, I was resisting being loved, and I was resisting myself.

Psalm 34 offers an invitation to "taste and see"[1] that God is good. We are designed to know God, trust his good purpose, and experience this knowing and trusting—in part through food.

After Jesus' resurrection, he invited his weary, downtrodden disciples to eat breakfast with him (John 21:1-14). He cooked fish and shared bread with his friends, taking the time for feeding both their bodies and their faith. His actions were a reminder of how he'd fed them before, connecting the dots between his provision and their togetherness.

Can you imagine the way the fish smelled as it cooked over an open fire, easing their doubts and tickling all their saddened senses toward hope? Or how the disciples would have remembered other times when they were hungry for that same breakfast and waited with anticipation, their stomachs growling? Perhaps they remembered such a meal being prepared by their mothers or fathers, or how they fed their own families the same way. Maybe they recalled the way Jesus took the five loaves and two fish and fed thousands, transforming the little they could see into more than enough, releasing them from their fear of scarcity and calming their worried hearts.

Then and now, Jesus opens our eyes and shows us how to recognize him, ourselves, and each other through the sharing of bread and the ministry of everything savory, spicy, and sweet.

———————◆———————

On my first trip to Korea, when I was seven, my parents let me stay overnight with one of my mom's cousins while they went to another city to search for my mom's baby brother. Before she left, my mom reminded me how to ask for water and how to say I needed the bathroom in Korean. The rest was left to hand motions and my Pictionary skills. Then she squatted down in front of me, holding my elbows in her hands. She stared into my eyes and said, "You eat whatever they give you for breakfast tomorrow. No faces. Just swallow, drink water, say thank you. No picky."

I forgot about her instructions until the next morning. My mom's cousin, who I called Imo ("auntie"), asked me if I was hungry. Remembering what my mom told me, I peered into the kitchen for clues about what she might be serving. There were no boxes of cereal in sight.

She smiled, headed to the kitchen, and came out with a small white bowl. Inside was rice with a fish on top, followed by a raw egg, its yolk dripping down the sides of the bowl. I swallowed. I'd never eaten an entire fish before, or a raw egg.

But I could still see my mom's stern face in the back of my mind, so I gulped it down quickly.

"Gamsahamnida," I said, smiling at my imo with a slight bow of my head. Then I asked her for mul. I gulped down the entire glass of water and smiled at her when I was done.

At the time, I thought this was just a moment I needed to endure. But when I told my mom later how I'd eaten all of it without a fuss, she smiled in a way I'd never seen before. She told me that breakfast is what she would love to have every morning.

I realized I'd never thought about what kind of breakfast my mom grew up eating—or how often she didn't get to have what she wanted. For a moment, I peered beyond the layer of who she'd always been to me—my mom, the one who gave me what I needed—and noticed that she was human and had tastes and desires just like I did. For the first time, I truly saw her. I'd found something I didn't even know was lost between us.

Jesus was at work bringing about cultural redemption over a simple breakfast meal in Incheon, the way he had at the Sea of Galilee thousands of years before. When Jesus revealed his resurrected self to the disciples on that melancholy morning, he did it not only by miraculously feeding them but also by reminding them that he was with them in every part of their humanity. Despite the shock and awe of his death-conquering deity, he made a meal.

◆

Years later, I sat on a white plastic lawn chair with a plateful of food in front of me. I sat there talking and passing dishes by candlelight. The power had gone out again in the little house where we were staying on the shore of Lake Kivu in Rwanda. Our ministry team was visiting a beautiful coffee plantation that sprawled across the hills near the lakeshore.

I listened to the tiny dance of waves through the open windows while taking my first bite of a fish that had been caught by a local fisherman. Just a few hours earlier, the fisherman had pulled his small boat onto the shore. He had retrieved a machete half the size of my body to cut down a collection of fish from the ropes they were tied to.

I carefully worked through the slivers of bones with my fork, bypassing the head. In the dark, I listened to our host, my new friend, tell me how he'd eaten this specific dish of fish and potatoes with his family when he was young. He'd lost that family in the Rwandan genocide. And now he was serving my American friends and me the same meal, along with that story and treasure of a memory.

I savored the unfamiliar taste of this fish from the lake behind me before I swallowed, remembering my mom's instruction from decades before, thankful I had experience eating things I didn't know. I understood then that these offerings of food pass through a holy umbilical cord that connects all of us, reminding us that we belong to one another, beyond our own brokenness and our limitations of flavor and food. We don't have to lick clean the unfamiliar bowls we're offered wherever we go, but if we can, why wouldn't we?

Despite my love for tteokguk as a girl, I didn't know anything about it. I didn't know until I was much older that it's the soup Koreans eat for Lunar New Year. I only knew I couldn't get enough of spoon-searching for the chewy white ovals in my bowl, and that seemed like enough. But no matter how many soupy rice cakes I consumed during my childhood, I was missing so many details that millions of other Koreans knew.

I started making tteokguk for my family a few years ago. Each time it feels like an act of resistance, rebuilding, and redemption. And each time I stand over the pot, measuring the guk-ganjang and letting the tteok sit in a bath of cold water, I hear shouts and whispers suggesting I'm a fake. It's as if the friend who said she doesn't think of me as Asian, the classmates who demanded I tell them where I was from while guessing anywhere but Korea, the Korean boy who poked me with a toothpick, and the spitting teenagers in Haeundae have banded together, uttering derogatory comments about my claim to being Korean.

The first time I made a version of the soup I was proud of, my kids sat around the table, excited. They liked the idea that the white slices of chewy deliciousness symbolize a fresh start for the new year, and that they resembled the moon. Then one of them complained about the egg slices. Another whined about the green onions, and another would drink only the broth.

I sent my mom a picture of the soup in our family Messenger app, hoping she would approve of what it looked like and wouldn't respond with questions about why it looked so dark (like last year, when I used the wrong kind of soy sauce) or whether I'd forgotten a key ingredient.

I opened the app again and again, checking for her response.

Thirty minutes later, my phone dinged and a message popped up: "Looks good! We are on our way!"

My kids came close to the phone, wanting to see what she said. They took her message seriously, thinking their grandparents were coming to visit. I had to explain that she was only expressing a desire to come and eat tteokguk with us.

I imagined my kids as adults, wondering what journey each of them would travel as they rejected or embraced their own ethnic identity. Would they try to make tteokguk for Lunar New Year with their kids? Would they get together and eat it? Would they find a Korean restaurant and order it? Would they forget about the holiday altogether?

God, maker of our tongues and our taste buds, I prayed silently, *help these three to taste and see that you are good—the loving Creator of their every part. Use this food and these memories to help them know your love, taste it, remember it, and offer it to those they will love, nourish, and nurture someday.*

CHAPTER 5

STRANGERS
AND SCARS

No one ever told me that grief felt so like fear.

C. S. LEWIS

I was six when I found out my sister and I didn't have the same father. I was six when I realized that someone could be married more than once. I was six when I started asking a lot of questions about how families are made and how they fall apart.

We hadn't been living in Tokyo for very long. After we spent three years in California, one year in Wisconsin, and another in New York, my dad eagerly volunteered to move our family of four overseas, knowing we would be that much closer to Korea, that much closer to my mom's home and all her missing pieces.

Families often make decisions in search of missing pieces. Whether it's a conscious choice or not, loss drives us toward one fork in the road over another. Our four years in Japan were like that for us. It was a time of undoing and further mixing, a time when our family went through the wash and came out on the other side a bit wrinkled and forever different.

I stood at the edge of our narrow kitchen hours after I'd gone to bed. The arguing had woken me. I shuffled down the hall in my button-down pajamas, groggy but curious and worried. We'd been woken by earthquakes often since moving there, but this time only familiar voices were shaking.

All I heard clearly was my sister, Cathy, stating, "I'm going to move back to the States to live with my dad."

Standing in the dark shadows of the hall, I asked if our family was breaking in half. My mom, dad, and sister paused, surprised to see me awake.

Then my dad said, "Don't worry. Go back to bed."

To this day, I struggle to remember the weeks after that night. I don't know what I said to my sister or what my sister or my parents explained to me the next morning. I remember what Cathy wore at the airport when she left: a black and white herringbone coat that went to her ankles.

I brought my stuffed panda bear with sad eyes and

told her my panda didn't want her to go. I couldn't tell her it was really me who didn't want her to leave, because a rejection of my stuffed animal was sad, yes, but manageable. I didn't know how to face a rejection of me as a sister.

I watched her leave, regardless of how sad my panda bear was. And with barely an ounce of understanding about what was happening or why, I believed it was all my fault.

We left the Narita airport as three, plus one sad bear. When we returned home, I went straight to Cathy's teenage room. In the past, she hadn't allowed me inside, but that day, in the aftermath of losing her, I sat there for hours. I pulled her Duran Duran T-shirt over my head, on top of my pink and green sweater.

I sat on the floor of her room, looking for clues. I read through her school notebooks and studied her handwriting, gripping everything in my lap as if someone or something might come at any moment to snatch it all away.

After that, much of my childhood was spent alone. I played with dolls in the basement playroom. I watched my favorite cartoon, *Doraemon*, while my mom cooked dinner, lost in dialogue I didn't understand, simultaneously comforted and angered by it.

Weather permitting, my mom sometimes let me

wander around the neighborhood on foot or by bicycle. For such a big city, Tokyo is safe. I wandered on busy sidewalks and empty streets, always alone, always on the outside looking in. I was familiar with the view from the other side of the glass.

Those four years of living overseas as a kid, and especially the time after my sister left, provided training in silent observation, teaching me to become someone who notices things.

———————◆———————

I think Moses was also someone who noticed things.

Moses was forty when he began to publicly connect with his ethnic identity. In the book of Exodus, we get a glimpse into his story, starting when his life was spared by being adopted into an Egyptian royal family. We don't get much detail about what it would have been like for Moses, an Israelite, to be raised by Egyptian royalty, but I imagine he must have had a wide range of emotions bound up within his embodied, dual-cultured life. When he saw an Egyptian man mistreating a Hebrew slave, he reacted in anger and took the Egyptian man's life.[1]

It would be another forty years in the wilderness—in a completely different culture—before we hear about Moses wrestling with his own identity.

As a new father, Moses named his firstborn son Gershom, meaning "foreigner," because Moses had been a "foreigner in a foreign land" (Exodus 18:3). I can imagine how heavily the weight of foreignness must have fallen on Moses' shoulders—heavily enough to wrap his son's identity in that significant part of his own. *Hello, my name is Sojourner and Stranger.*

He named his next son Eliezer, saying, "The God of my ancestors was my helper; he rescued me from the sword of Pharaoh" (Exodus 18:4). One son carried the weight of Moses' foreignness. Another son carried the remembrance of God's rescue as Moses ran away from home.

Moses' story is full of familial fracture, loss, loneliness, wandering, brokenness, and dual-cultured struggles, but also a God who pursued him—not after all these colliding details were resolved, but right in the middle of them. His ancestors, his cultural identity, his faith, and his own relationship with God are woven together with the making of his own family and the generations to come.

When I see Moses' fear and rage, and the way he ran away, I see myself. When I read about his encounter with a God he didn't yet know and his hesitation and insecurity over following God's lead, I remember my own hesitation and hiding. When I consider his worry that no one from his birth culture would listen to him or believe him, despite his being well spoken and successful in the Egyptian culture he was adopted into (Acts 7:22), I can relate. When I imagine his feelings of being in between worlds and cultures, I feel a little closer to whole.

I wonder about when Moses was forced to leave his sister because of the brokenness and sin of others. I think about how Pharaoh's hard heart and narcissistic leadership must have traveled into Moses' story. Did Pharaoh mock him for the ways he resembled the Hebrews instead of the Egyptians? No matter how assimilated he was, his birth culture would have spoken through his skin color, his hair texture, and the shape of his eyes. I am sure he would have been lonely. His privilege and his assimilation into Egyptian culture separated him from his birth culture; his origin and his irrevocable Hebrew ties separated him from his adoptive culture.

It's liberating for me to realize Moses wasn't asked to deny his ethnic and cultural identity to know God and lead others. In fact, it was the opposite. His ability to understand both Hebrews and Egyptians meant he was uniquely qualified to lead a diverse group of people into the future. He was able to carry tensions and consider angles that others might not naturally think about.

When God first introduced himself to Moses through a burning bush, he announced that he was the God of Moses' father, meaning his Hebrew father (Exodus 3:6). God connected the dots of Moses' life, starting with his birth culture, and named himself from that reference point. Moses was forced to leave his family of origin because the systems of the world he lived in would not support him or a family like his. He was a target, yet God made a way for him to flourish in a culture that initially wanted to crush him. Throughout Moses' journey, he lived in a liminal, in-between space. There was nowhere he could go, no identity he could choose for himself—every space contained loss and grief. No matter how far he fled, every place led him back to his two worlds: the one he was born into and the one he was raised in.

We carry the stories of our families alongside God's intentional redemption of those stories. Moses named his first son "foreigner," and Gershom would indeed become a stranger and sojourner. But the redemption reflected in his second son's name would also lead all of us strangers and sojourners to know that we're not alone.

God uses our family names and stories, even the shameful parts, to lead us to shalom.

———————◆———————

The year after Cathy left Japan, I would still look for evidence of her in the school halls. I attended a private school for international students, and when my small elementary class walked to the high school building to use the gym, I would look for her even though I knew she wasn't there.

Shortly after this time, I started stealing.

It started at a sleepover with a friend. We walked from her house to a convenience store dressed in hats—"to disguise ourselves," as she instructed. For the sheer thrill of getting away with taking something that wasn't ours, we sneaked candies into our small pockets and left giggling. We ran all the way to the closest park to stuff our faces.

At that age, I didn't think about whether it was wrong. The rush of it distracted me from what I was feeling and from what had happened with my sister that no one would explain to me. In a way I couldn't have articulated at the time, I decided that being distracted would keep me from sinking.

After that first experience, I moved on to stealing little things on my own: a classmate's eraser, a Snoopy pencil box left outside at recess, a sheet of stickers, a box of cough drops, and a few origami sheets more than we were supposed to take for art class.

The small items added up, one by one, like secrets filling the empty space where something had been taken from me. Stealing shook away my feelings of guilt and grief and dressed them up with excitement. The fleeting distraction of this feelings-dress-up kept me looking for more things to take and keep.

Until the phone rang one evening, and I got caught.

Our Japanese landlords knew I was lonely after my sister left, and connected our family with a family that lived around the corner. The siblings who lived there— one older and one younger than me—invited me to their apartment on the third floor after school one day.

We met outside, and they showed me how they get into their apartment with a key stored in a basket just outside the door. We shuffled into the apartment and found the snacks their mom had left out for us on a counter. She came home shortly after we had eaten our snacks and took us to the roof of the building, where there were tables and toys. We had trouble communicating, but I left happier than I'd been in a long time.

The next day after school, I told my mom that my new friends said I could come over again that afternoon. That wasn't exactly accurate, but to be fair, they *had* said, "Let's play again soon." At that age, soon means the next day.

I ran from our home to their apartment complex and up the three flights of stairs. I found their door, thinking about the snacks we'd eaten the day before and how we'd played together on the roof.

I pressed my finger against the doorbell. After the echoing buzz, there was no response. I waited. I pressed it again, holding down my finger as if my energy alone could summon my friends to the door.

More silence. I pressed the bell long and hard one more time. A woman next door peeked out, shook her head at me, then shut the door.

I decided not to ring the bell again. But I remembered where they kept the key, and I felt some pull of power.

I left with the key and ran down three flights of stairs, clutching it tightly in my fist. I came out into the noise and air of the city, struck awake from my fog of anger. I barely knew these new friends, but I was angry that they weren't there when I thought they would be.

Even at that young age, my body wanted to release the sadness within me in a physical way. My anger wasn't really about them or our miscommunication; I was angry that my sister was gone when I thought she shouldn't be. I was sad for all the mature things that were lost in translation in my young mind—why she was gone, what had happened to lead up to this.

When I stood at that door and no one answered, emotions filled my body like a tsunami. I looked at the key in my hand, now slippery and wet with sweat, and I panicked. I had no plan beyond taking it. I squatted in the shadows around the corner from the apartment building and started digging with my small fingers in a stretch of dirt. I buried the key, my anger, and my grief in the dark soil.

Weeks after I dug in the dirt, my parents got a phone call from the landlords. My mom and dad took turns on the phone and talked to each other in hushed tones, glancing at me while I watched *Doraemon*, eyes fixed on the screen. I stole quick glances at them with ears wide open.

They hung up and looked at each other, turned off the TV, and faced me. They told the story from the point of view of my new friends' family and shared all the havoc wreaked by my impulsive action.

My dad looked straight into my eyes and asked me if I had taken the key. I lied, shoving the rising heat deep inside. I dug deeper and deeper within, wondering how much further down the truth could be buried before there was nowhere left for it to go.

After stealing the key and lying about it, I learned

to trust in my ability to hide. I decided my belovedness was earned by goodness, and my goodness was maintained by my ability to hide the ugly parts inside.

If I'd been born into the same time period and culture as Gershom and Eliezer, I wonder what my name would have been. What would I be reminded that I carry every time I told someone my name?

---◆---

In the months after Cathy returned to the States, I began to ask my mom questions. Each one led to another: "But when did you actually come to America?" "How did you get to California?" "Where was Cathy?" "Why didn't you bring her with you?" "What happened?" "Who is her father?"

Bit by bit, pieces of our story unraveled, revealing shame, trauma, and brokenness. My mom didn't want my sister or me to carry any of it, but the more hidden the truth, the more the shame passes on from one generation to the next.

I didn't fully comprehend how my mom could have had a life before she knew my dad. It felt wrong, and I wanted constant confirmation that her life now was better, that she wasn't going to leave us too.

After my sister moved, we sent each other letters. I would tell her that I missed her and ask if she was going to visit for the summer. I stopped telling my friends that I had a sister who was a black belt in karate because I didn't know how to explain where she was, and sometimes a friend would accuse me of lying and tell me they thought I'd made her up.

I spent recess alone, wandering from the monkey bars to a seesaw with no one on the other end. I would jump on a merry-go-round for a few spins, then leave dizzy, looking for someone to play with. I found moments of quiet from my own anxiety by hiding in a bathroom stall for a few minutes longer than I needed. I looked for the playground clock, hoping that the hands would say it was almost time to go inside, where I could leave my loneliness behind for a few hours.

I was only seven or eight years old, yet I grew accustomed to living in a social wilderness. I was thirsty for help, but I didn't know how to ask for it.

It's been over thirty years since that late-night revelation, and now my sister and I live in the same county. We're both married, we're both moms, and we've lived twenty-five minutes away from one another for the last ten years—the longest time we've ever lived this close. Between my grade school years and now, we had little pockets of time together: a summer vacation in Korea, random visits here and there.

And there was a year she lived with us while going

to college nearby. I loved that year. She defended me to Mom and Dad when I wanted to cover my wall with magazine pictures or go to a friend's house. Sometimes she drove me around or picked me up, sparing me from my parents and their barrage of questions. She always had cool music and funny things to say.

We talked about our parents, and she understood things that none of my other friends did. I asked her about her dad and the rest of her family, who were all strangers to me, as I tried to understand them and see them from her point of view.

The more I heard her side of the story, the more I felt like I should know the family she had that wasn't mine, while at the same time not wanting anything to do with them. I harbored judgment and blamed them for the hurt I saw in my mom, and the distance between my sister and me. The more I learned, the more I placed the blame on someone else instead of myself.

Sometimes the family story we've been given feels unfamiliar, like a dance we don't know. It takes time, mistakes, and starting over again. Loss must be felt. Grief needs expression. Anxiety tells a story. Confusion needs clarification and comfort. Feelings need somewhere to go. And healing requires space, tenderness, and time. Sometimes you have to get to know each other again or survive being apart, whether that's because of boundaries you create or separations you can't control.

But in and around it all, there's grace. That grace is enough, and when we let it be enough, surrender is possible; glimpses of shalom are visible.

———————◆———————

After graduating from college and then doing full-time college ministry in Germany for two years, I moved home with my parents for a short stint. They'd opened a restaurant while I was away—their small Asian restaurant/karaoke place was their newest kid. It was an imperfect dream come true for my mom.

The summer I moved home, I spent a lot of time there, helping my mom unload beverage deliveries, cleaning tables and bathrooms, and getting ready to open each day. I was shocked by how small the place was and what a toll it had taken on my parents. My mom had burn scars on her hands and fingers, she'd been robbed at knifepoint earlier that year, she'd hit unruly customers over the head with a frying pan to make them leave when they were bothering other customers, she drank with her friends and customers, and she'd lost so much weight from the work and stress that she resembled a small girl.

I wanted her to have her dream, but I couldn't bear

to see her that way. I called my sister, who drove out to visit. She and I weren't close at that point, but she was the only one who could understand.

We drove to the restaurant together. It was late, and the place was filled with drunk customers. We sat in the parking lot spying on our mom, ready to help her if she needed it. We stayed in that dark lot for hours, watching and waiting, holding the broken dreams of our mom between us, ready to catch the pieces.

At times the distance between my sister and me has felt great and the path to each other impassable. Yet moments like this remind me that we are bound not only by our Korean mother's womb and blood but by the shattered dreams we help carry and mend.

Sometimes I think about how a family legacy is passed from one generation to the next. The one I've been given was tattered and torn before it reached me. I've carried it through the world with shame, yet God's redemption bell rings to remind me that he didn't come to earth for the righteous who have no need. He came for the ragamuffins and the ones who feel ridiculous. He came to bridge broken relation-ships and gaps I never would be able to cross on my own. He came for fractured families—for my family and for the stories I've been too embarrassed to tell. His mercy is the tie between us all, and even when it seems like there's no hope or path forward, he carries me.

God's mercy is wider than the fractures in my family. His redemption is stronger than the sins of our past and the habits we can't seem to shake. I always thought my job was to stop the sin patterns and go a different way, like some kind of hero. And while I do believe I can be part of communal, familial repentance in our family line, I'm beginning to see that this isn't because I'm better than those who came before me; it's because I'm desperate enough to ask for help.

Where we begin matters, and there's no beginning where God's grace doesn't reach. His grace can reach my sister, me, and all the parts lost between us—and the parts that stretch far beyond us in our family tree.

My sister and I don't usually send each other Hallmark-style "sister mugs," but we've driven together down quiet highways in the middle of the night, passing nothing but semis, to make sure our mom is okay. We've called each other about how to celebrate Mom's seventieth birthday, understanding the layers of loss in our stories.

Our story isn't typical, and our family tree isn't symmetrical, but it's the story God has given us, and when I look at it through the eyes of mercy, it is breathtakingly beautiful.

The house my family and I live in came with a large yard that backs up to a property outside our neighborhood. Barbed wire separates our yard from this wild, tree-filled land, and the trees reach over the fence into our yard. They are tangled and covered with vines, and the dirt on our side is covered in weeds, dead leaves, sticks, and empty walnut shells.

When we moved in, my husband and I were overwhelmed by what it would take to clean and care for the yard. But we've been out there every day we can since the weather has warmed up, trying to believe we can care for what's been given to us. Matt spent months researching different kinds of plants and invasive weeds, figuring out what to do about moles, finding the best tools for landscaping, and clearing out the yard, section by section. It has been a long, mostly unseen, labor of love.

Sometimes our family stories feel too scandalous and scarred for us to believe they can offer the world anything good. But that work of clearing debris, removing one weed after another, is holy, tenderhearted work. The land we occupy is the same land God spoke into being with his own breath. When we work it, we partake in the same redemption story that began after Adam and Eve were banished from the Garden of Eden and then given another way toward shalom. Some parts of our story may never tidy up the way we've been told family relationships are supposed to. But once we let go of that "supposed to," we can build from where we are.

No matter your family history, Jesus has been there. He knows what it's like to be born into a family that sometimes thinks you are crazy. He knows what it's like to lose family and to have scandalous branches in your family tree. Jesus, the ultimate healer, knows that familial healing is often anything but instant—not something that can be summed up on a coffee mug.

There's nothing you can uncover in your legacy that will separate you or your family from God's love. There's no story you can tell that will keep you from God's goodness. That thing that has convinced you to run and hide until you're left unconnected in the wilderness—it can't stop God from pursuing you and loving you, along with every branch in your family.

We are not the saviors of our families, nor are we the ones meant to carry the full weight of their broken branches. We are those whose desperation for Jesus in the midst of our families' brokenness creates paths of healing.

When I was six, I found out that families can fall apart. When I was six, my family's own Garden of Eden was shattered. I understood then that fruit could be eaten when it wasn't supposed to be, that consequences would follow, and that hearts would be broken beyond what seemed reparable at the time.

When I was six, I discovered it's possible to begin a long journey away from what *was* to look for what could be. Since then, I've slowly been learning that the family God gave me hasn't been banished from what was, left to ourselves to figure out how to hold our brokenness together. In all the years before and since, my family has been in God's hands, and God has been working to mend the ripped-open and worn-out seams.

CHAPTER 6

SHALOMSICK

Christian spirituality involves a transformation of the self that
occurs only when God and self are both deeply known. Both,
therefore, have an important place in Christian spirituality. There
is no deep knowing of God without a deep knowing of self,
and no deep knowing of self without a deep knowing of God.

DAVID G. BENNER

Finding a church home was impossible for my family
when I was growing up. Aside from an Asian American
church we attended for a few years while we lived in
California, we were never able to find a place that
felt like home. It wasn't only because of how often we
moved, including stints overseas, but because, as Martin
Luther King Jr. said, Sunday at 11:00 a.m. is "the most
segregated hour in this nation."

When we lived in Japan, our family tried a large
American church, but we attended on only a handful

of occasions. It took a long time to get there, and even though we were in an Asian country, most of the Americans who attended weren't Asian American. None of the other families looked like ours, or lived like ours. During our time in Indiana, we tried Korean churches, but no one except my mom understood what was going on.

My mom taught me about reverence, desperation, and surrender before I heard white male pastors talk about it or white evangelical worship bands sing about it, with hands raised high. Rather than attending a traditional church with four walls and Sunday school, I spent most Sundays at home. And yet I have deeply embedded memories of watching my mom watch what she called "Jesus movies."

Looking back at my "unchurched" years—the ones I thought (and was taught) were only wilderness and desert—I see that this season actually held lessons in humility, desperation, and worship. The lessons I learned from my mom about who Jesus is made their way into my heart, long before I knew how to rearticulate them or even realized how much I was learning from watching her.

She taught me holy stories with her tears as she watched Jesus on-screen in *Ben-Hur*. No matter how many creative liberties were taken with the Jesus she watched, she sat still and cried with longing for him—sometimes with knees bent on the ground. Everything stopped when he was on-screen.

She taught me that Jesus was the obvious and only answer to her nightmares and heartache. She brought all her pain to our television screen, like her own alabaster jar. She carried it from her past and passed down to me all her promises and personal desires—everything.

The first time I read the story of the woman who broke open her jar of perfume at Jesus' feet, as well as the story of the woman at the well and the story of the bleeding woman, it was my mother's face, my mother's tears, my mother's desperation, my mother's humility that I pictured. I saw women with my mom's face, eyes, slender hands, dark hair, and burdened heart. These women carried years of pain and trauma that reached back further than their own lives, yet they were loved, sought after, seen, and healed by Jesus.[1]

Without any words, tidy booklets, or sermons, I knew deep down there was only one answer to all this heartache and weight. I could see these women clearly because I was the daughter of a woman like them. She had modeled those things to me in our living room while an oily Charlton Heston appeared on our TV.

So when Grandma Margie sat me down in the armchair just inside the front door of my grandparents'

Arroyo Grande home and shared a booklet with me about Jesus, I already knew I needed him. I knew I needed a Savior, because my mom had modeled that need and told me that Jesus was the only one who could answer it. As I prayed with my grandma, my thighs sticking to the armchair while she kneeled beside me, I pictured my mom crying out to on-screen Jesus with her whole being.

◆

As scientists continue to learn about epigenetics, there's more and more evidence that trauma can be passed from one generation to the next. The study of inter-generational trauma is helping to inform us about the long-lasting impacts of starvation, poverty, war, extreme stress, abuse, and other scarring life experiences.

In her book *Survivor Café*, author Elizabeth Rosner writes, "We will embody the DNA of the dead." In other words, our generation's DNA "carries the expression of our parents' trauma, and the trauma of our grand-parents' too. Our own biochemistry and neurology have been affected by what they endured. Epigenetics researchers are looking at the ways that the experiences of starvation, grief, and shock pass forward into the future."[2]

In Korean culture, epigenetics is assumed without a

long scientific name or explanation. Han has been part of Asian culture, and Korean culture in particular, for centuries. In many Asian countries, it's understood that human suffering and sadness attach themselves to the heart and womb, passing this sadness or trauma from one generation to the next.

In countries and people groups that have collectively experienced one traumatic experience after another, we find evidence of epigenetics, or han, at work in the children and children's children of those who have lived through oppression, systemic injustice, racism, poverty, and war. These experiences of trauma passed through generations—and the han we carry—are not given by God as a means to an end. But what if they are the soil God uses to show us our need for Jesus and open us to love?

I am the daughter of a Korean immigrant, and the great-granddaughter of Dutch immigrants. I am a daughter of war, poverty, oppression, invasion, loss, and colonization. When we are born, we are born with a history. We are not book one in our own series. We are stories in a long, connected saga. Remembering the books that came before our own is essential to our health, the health of our homes, the health of our communities, and the health of our faith and spirituality.

On the collective experience of Koreans, Andrew Sung Park writes, "Koreans all throughout history have been continually invaded by surrounding countries. As a relatively small country, Korea has been the prey of its powerful neighbors. As a result Koreans have acquired a dejected spirit of life. Their music, poetry, drama, and linguistic expression indicate a han-filled spirit. In the English expression, 'a bird sings,' but in Korean, 'a bird cries.'"[3]

There's a reason why a well-fed, perfectly clothed little girl like me could feel some of the weight of things I never carried myself. Before my mom told me the stories of her past, I felt them in her songs and in my own body. I am linked to my history, and I carry this history into the future.

◆

In grade school, my friend Bethany invited me to her Eastern Orthodox church. Both of us were mixed-race Asian American girls born a decade after the civil rights movement to parents who lived through it: her parents were sixties hippies; mine, a Navy man and a Korean immigrant. Together we searched for God and an understanding of ourselves, with the backdrop of *E.T.*, LA Gear, and *Sweet Valley Twins*. Even then, I somehow knew that these seemingly disconnected parts of my identity were deeply connected to my faith journey in ways no one ever explained to me.

From the moment I walked into the small sanctuary, I thought I would choke from the scent of incense. The smell was heavy, like a coat worn in the wrong season. Bethany told me excitedly about the special oils that burned the way they did centuries ago, carrying on the traditions of the early church and connecting us with another time. She pointed out the icons on the wall, each one in dark, muted colors—melancholy, haunting, and beautiful.

At that age, I was already familiar with sadness. I had no desire to find it on the walls of a church or search for it in painted faces with suffering eyes. Sorrow wasn't an abstract reminder for me—it was the reality I woke up to. I found it in the eyes of my mom while she made me breakfast each day.

I held my coughing in until I could no longer contain it and it poured out of me like a siren, announcing my awkward presence in this holy place.

I wondered how I could ever fit in somewhere if the special offering to God made my throat scratchy and my breathing uncomfortable. The choir music was beautiful and melancholy, like the icons, but I didn't know how to join in. I couldn't keep up with the music or sing along. When it was time for the Eucharist, I knew I was supposed to stay in my seat. My friend had explained it to me numerous times—I wasn't allowed to partake because I wasn't Eastern Orthodox.

Her family stepped over my knobby knees and filed out of the row we sat in. They waited in line and slowly walked the front, where tall men stood in robes, one holding a cup of wine and another placing a piece of bread in each congregant's mouth. I watched each person kiss the priest's hairy hand before their turn with the wine and then the bread. I was glad I didn't have to join them in being fed by a stranger and kissing his knuckle. But I also felt my cheeks burn as I sat in that row alone, staring at my shoes. I decided they weren't dressy enough to be in that room.

My friend's older brother squeezed back into our row, smiled at me, then quickly handed me a warm, squishy piece of bread he'd managed to grab. It was a warmth offered under the table, and it was the first time I felt welcomed and included that morning. I held the piece of bread in my fist for the rest of the service, squeezing it until it became something like dough again.

Jesus is clear about who he welcomes: everyone. He's clear about who longs for shalom and who shalom is meant for: everyone. He modeled the limitlessness of compassion, and the way grace knows no boundaries, like a forceful river that won't be told what to do or where to go.

Grace and compassion are fluid powers we often try to tame because of our own fears about how far they may take us beyond what we know or understand. But what if this kind of limitless compassion is cut loose in our lives and changes things? What if it asks us to rebuild a foundation to replace the one we've become attached to and comfortable with? What if it asks us to serve someone we don't even want to look in the eye? What if it removes the false security of our knowing, our traditions, our reputation, our power, or our titles?

When we acknowledge our own pain, we learn to see the pain of others. When we are willing to accept the ache in our own hearts, we are capable of welcoming the ache we find in others. When we welcome the hurt we find in others, we are able to see the world and ourselves in a new way and understand that our own view is limited.

Bethany is Japanese American—biracial, Asian American, like me. When I moved from the bustling city of Tokyo to the laid-back, coastal-cool city of Goleta, we noticed each other right away. I recognized her wide, double-lidded eyes that "kiss in the corners."[4] We had the same mix of Asian and European hair, each strand confused by a desire to be textured and silky straight. The *both/and* phrase is a reality of mixed-race lives from the moment we're born.

Bethany and I knew right away there were things we shared, and even if we couldn't articulate the inherent sadness that accompanies growing up with an internal clash of cultures and learning to navigate the systems in the cultures we lived in, we felt it. And we found safety in acknowledging some of those feelings together.

———◆———

When I was in fifth grade, my parents suggested I go to an Asian American summer camp. I didn't want to go, but they were united in their belief that a week with other Asian American kids in the mountains of Northern California would help me in the ways I most needed it.

After two summers at camp, I knew Bethany needed to come too. So one June day when we were in seventh grade, Bethany and I, along with a few others from a local church, made the trek to Northern California to meet God with kids who looked like us under the tall pine trees of Mount Hermon.

At camp, we giggled over our commonalities with the other campers—things like a love for Sanrio products, our dark heads of hair, and taking selfies before selfies were a thing. We listened to leaders who looked like our moms, relieved that we never had to explain "what we were" or what we ate at home. Having these ordinary details in common in the midst of worship sessions and small group sharing time felt like a home-coming I didn't know how to articulate; I just knew I never wanted to leave. I longed for this experience to be my everyday life.

When camp came to an end, Bethany and I cried, but we were glad we would be able to reminisce together. We'd get our rolls of film developed at a pharmacy, and once the stacks of photos came in, we'd spend hours looking through them, talking about our friends, the boys we liked, and what it was like to deepen our faith with kids who looked like us.

It was at camp that Bethany and I found a sense of home while also facing a new kind of loneliness. As two of the few biracial campers, we didn't fully fit in there, but we knew we didn't fit in back home, either. We talked about how to get better at fitting in with the Asian American community we'd fallen in love with.

On the last day of camp, we rushed around getting our new friends to sign our camp photo. I wondered if leaving camp that day also meant leaving behind my hope for a faith that was integrated with my Asian American experience. Maybe it was hiding in the grass somewhere in the middle of Mount Hermon, where the summer sun shines and everything feels like it might have a place just out of my reach—but I could visit it sometimes, like Narnia.

When we packed our sleeping bags and duffel bags at the end of camp one year, I remember how they lined the back of the conference room, with a pillow on top of each bag like icing on a cupcake. I was sad to go home, because being in this place felt like home now. It was my first time being surrounded by other Asian American kids. It was the first time the adults leading me, from cabin counselors to speakers, were all Asian American.

When my parents arrived to pick me up, I didn't worry about what my mom would say or how her words would sound when she talked to my new friends. They understood. They respected her. They saw her. She was like their own moms. I left with my pillow under my arm, simultaneously floating toward feeling unknown and looking over my shoulder remembering the feeling of being known.

Though I went to camp kicking and screaming, it turned out that being there with kids who looked like me, learning to sing "Pharaoh, Pharaoh" with hand motions, was medicine for my lonely, searching soul.

After camp, I exchanged letters with my new friends. They wrote on Sanrio stationery with perfect lettering—years before lettering became a thing non-Asian women made money on. I invested in stationery and started practicing my handwriting for hours every week.

Most of them went to school or church together, or even played on the same basketball team. They lived in communities where being Asian American didn't make them feel like a minority. Their experience of being Asian American was completely different from mine.

One summer during high school, after we'd moved to Indiana, I flew out to stay with Bethany for a few weeks so we could attend camp together. After camp, we lay on her bed surrounded by packs of Kodak photos, listening to the Cowboy Junkies on repeat. We talked about this person or that one, about boys and leaders, about funny and embarrassing moments, and about all the things that weren't that we wished could be. We talked about nightmares, demons, and Jesus. We wondered if we would ever feel comfortable in our own Asian American bodies, and we wished parts of those bodies away.

We searched for identity together, with melancholy music playing, as I stared at an icon of Mary, Jesus' mother, hanging above her bed. We decided to try to pray together—for my family to move back to California, for our teenage crushes, for the Sun In to really work in our dark hair, for the hard parts of our families' stories, for the nightmares that kept revisiting us.

However selfish and misguided our prayers were, they were honest. We meant them, and we had no desire to sound holy. I was leaving to fly back to Indiana in a few days, and we'd have to leave the safety of that summer. The ache felt less severe and not as hard to explain when we were together. But once I went home, we'd be left to face that longing alone. It wasn't just camp or our in-person friendship that we'd miss—it was the integration of our journeys of faith and identity that we couldn't find in other places.

Jesus said that where two or more are gathered, he is there.[5] It was the ache for shalom, shared in our most honest and whole selves, that not only connected us to each other but carried us to the feet of Jesus, together.

My journey of embracing my ethnic and cultural identity has led me to Jesus and deepened my longing for the way things are meant to be. Programs and traditions may help us see or name the ache, but we need to feel it first.

The face staring back at me in the mirror that I once saw as too Asian and not Asian enough, as too dark or too light, eventually beckoned me toward the embrace of my whole self. Facing my ache for shalom begged me to ask whether we are loved and brave and broken, and then to sit still and wait for the God of the universe to answer.

I am in the church because now I know that I *am* the church too. The more I've embraced my own identity, the more I've come to understand who this bride of Christ is. Its beauty, power, and purposes are much wider than any building, denomination, style, generation, or people group can contain. While my family and I do attend a church building, I know church can happen in the exchange of squishy bread, in the offering of spoons of Korean stew, and in Western-style Jesus movies.

I grew up believing that something was wrong with my family—that if we just became more like the families I saw in majority white churches, we'd fit in. And though today there are many churches that call themselves "multiethnic" or have a vision of becoming such, my current mixed-race family still doesn't fit. We've found ways to belong outside those walls, but trying to force churches to get to a place they aren't has only led me to deep disappointment.

As I look back at those years filled with teenage pain and longings, it would be easy to brush it all off as a necessary part of that season of life. However, when we look closer and dig into the details, we can see that our longings lead us to our most pressing questions about who we are. These questions push us further down a path to whose we are.

Our shalomsickness hurts, but it's what reminds us of where we came from and where we're going. These pains of longing lead us home—from tiny homecomings along the way to the Home we've been created to journey toward with every part of our image-bearing selves.

CHAPTER 7

REMEMBRANCE AND HEALING

We are not makers of history; we are made by history.

MARTIN LUTHER KING JR.

The word *remember* shows up 253 times in the Bible. In Deuteronomy alone, it appears 16 times. Remembering is crucial to spiritual growth. God has always encouraged his people to remember where they came from and what he has done. God also tells us that he himself chooses to remember what he has done and what has happened between him and his people.

Remembering is both an act of love and a tool of survival. It's a choice made with future generations in mind. Remembering is a way we can both love the

Lord our God with our minds and love our neighbor as ourselves.

There's a Jewish tradition of reciting the Haggadah, the text that goes along with the Seder meal at Passover. In this text, there's a commandment that "every generation must retell the story of Exodus as if each of our souls were present alongside the enslaved Jews in Egypt."[1]

Imagine what it would be like if all people revisited their own histories this way. In doing so, we'd acknowledge the triumphal part of the past alongside the years of oppression, defeat, and wandering in the wilderness.

As we intentionally remember, we are unable to separate the two parts of our stories.

This type of remembering isn't done in a classroom while one person teaches and students sit at their desks, taking notes. It's done in community—around dinner tables, through storytelling and intentionality. There's a responsibility attached to this practice. It's not merely left to experts or religious teachers; the burden rests on families and relationships.

In Deuteronomy, God tells his people a number of times to remember him. He doesn't want them to forget that he's the one who helps them, leads them, and provides for them. In essence, he wants them to remember that they have come from dust and have nothing he didn't first give them in love.

Remembering this reality helps us to see the world with clear eyes and with God's heart. It moves us into a posture of dependence on him and surrender to the way he has made us.

Throughout his life and ministry, Jesus often asked questions that required people to remember. Jesus was a master at getting to the root of a person's memories and heart. Some refused to do the work it took to look back and turned away from his questions, choosing to leave them unanswered.

At the Passover meal, days before his crucifixion, Jesus served his disciples in the most tangible ways possible. He fed them dinner, and then he broke bread and passed around a shared cup of wine, telling his dear friends to keep doing this as an act of remembrance. *Do this to remember me. Keep living this way, like I've shown you. Use all your senses and cultural details to remember, remember, remember.* Bent below them, looking up at their faces and smelling the scents of every place they'd walked, he held their feet in his hands—the same hands he'd just eaten with—to clean them.[2]

Jesus knew how easy it is for us to forget. God knows what our minds are like—both their limitations and their ability to hold God-given power. He made our minds, and he has continually told us—his people throughout generations, cultures, and nations—to remember what he has done in our collective and individual histories.

————◆————

My junior year of high school, my friend Michelle invited me to go to youth group with her. She'd grown up going to church, but her family had stopped attending at some point. She said she felt a pull on her heart to go back.

I told her about the Asian American Christian camp I went to, and how much I missed those experiences in the mountains of Northern California. I remembered feeling a tug myself while at that camp, during bonfires and when we were asked to stand and recommit our lives to Jesus while someone played an acoustic guitar in the background.

I agreed to go with her. From the back parking lot, there was a path leading to what looked like a big barn-style house. We were late, and after we walked through the main area, we entered a room full of high schoolers singing worship songs. There was a small stage with more students singing and playing in the band.

I noticed two things right away. It felt similar to

those nights in the woods of Mount Hermon, with the same kinds of songs and with kids singing and closing their eyes or lifting their hands. But this time the kids looked nothing like me. I wondered then: maybe it didn't matter that I was the only Asian American. Maybe I could be at home here.

Weeks went by, and Michelle and I made friends and brought friends. Soon it was what we did every Sunday night.

I started meeting with the youth pastor's wife weekly. I'd go to her house and we'd chat while she cared for her kids, did dishes, and cleaned. We sat in the office at their house and prayed together before I left every week. She always asked me for prayer requests, but I never knew how to share mine.

Almost everything I wanted prayer for had to do with my relationship with my mom or struggles that were unique to our bicultural family. I never knew how to talk about those things or put words to them, because I didn't know anyone else who struggled in that way. There was no representation in my life throughout those years. So I asked her to pray for my parents to come to church.

Sure enough, they did. But when they stood outside after service, while groups of people gathered with friends and laughed, they remained close to the door.

I introduced them to a few of my friends and some adults I knew, but though the greetings were warm, an invisible wall separated them. It seemed like no one knew how to move beyond a quick handshake and hello, even me.

Meanwhile, youth group became everything to me. While I learned a lot about the Bible, grew in my faith, and treasured my time with the youth pastor's wife, it was also a time when I grew further and further away from my family. The deeper I grew in my relationships at church, the more my own upbringing and heritage didn't make sense.

When I tried to explain the tension I felt to a friend at youth group, he said, "I know another Asian guy who had a hard time too. His parents were so strict and demanding, and he came from all these Eastern beliefs."

I listened to his explanation, and though my insides were burning with anger, I didn't get to show it. I was embarrassed and confused. I wondered if it was my "Easternness" that was to blame for the division within me.

I led a little Bible study with younger high school girls, and one night we met in someone's home. One of the girls showed up late, after stopping somewhere else with another girl. Her mom found out and came to the house where we were meeting. She blamed me.

I'll never forget how she stuck her finger in my face, telling me, not her daughter, "This relationship is severed." Then she said, "I knew I shouldn't have trusted you."

We had no history, and I looked at the fair complexions and European features around the room. I couldn't prove it, then or now, but I felt targeted because of my Asian hair and skin—the traits that made me different from her and the other girls there.

———◆———

My last couple of years in college, I launched myself into ministry like it was my major. This experience differed from church and youth group, because I found a group of people who wanted to travel and explore the world like I did. For the first time, I was asked to go overseas, and I found other people who wanted to try new things and learn about other cultures. Their openness drew me in. I was discipled, and I discipled other women.

During my last year at school, I was torn between joining full-time ministry and furthering my education to pursue a dream of writing. My creative writing professor candidly asked me why I wouldn't pursue writing and why I couldn't do ministry and be a Christian while doing so. He told me that he remembered a Bible verse from his Roman Catholic childhood about not burying your gifts. Despite his advice, I left his office sure that I was supposed to let go of my dream of writing fiction "for the sake of the gospel."[3]

A few weeks later, I was giving a friend a ride across campus, and he asked me if I'd decided which country I wanted to apply to intern in for campus ministry. I told him Germany instead of Japan, where I'd done an internship the previous summer.

"Why would you choose Germany over the country where you lived as a kid and where you had such an amazing summer of ministry?" He shook his head. "Why wouldn't you want to go to an Asian country?"

He was being sincere, but his questions picked at the self-rejection in me.

I pushed back. "Just because I'm Asian doesn't mean I have to go to Asia."

The next fall I went to Germany. During my first year of full-time ministry, I met loads of students and talked to them about politics, culture, and Jesus. Most of them were interested in spirituality but uninterested in organized religion and the church. They knew the details of world history and the history of their own nations. They knew what can happen when people blindly follow charismatic leaders who promise to alleviate a nation's fears.

In our conversations, I talked about God's love with passion and faith, yet deep down, I wondered what it would feel like to believe I was not only loved but *wholly* loved.

I told no one about my doubts or the walls I faced. I'd come to a dead end. I was sure I was a fraud and an imposter, ready to unravel at the worst moment. It wasn't that I didn't believe in what I was doing or saying; I believed, and I felt like the dam holding back my fears and unbelief was about to break. Until I could let all the details of who I was unfold, I couldn't fully risk experiencing and knowing God's perfect love. I put on a brave spiritual face, but I was afraid of all the questions I had inside.

No one prepared me for this wall, this block between my Maker and me. Everyone, myself included, said it didn't matter—that being made new and having my identity in Christ was all that mattered. Ethnicity was a side dish, a means to the end goal of sharing the gospel—nothing more.

On my birthday, a particularly hot day in Freiburg toward the end of my first year there, I made gun mandu for my friends. I spent the days beforehand riding the bus and walking German streets, looking for the items I needed to cook Korean food. I searched two Indian grocery stores, navigating German and Indian culture to find things that resembled Korean ingredients. It felt impossible.

Finally, after searching through multiple stores, I found the closest thing I could to dumpling skins. They were the wrong shape and not quite the same, but they would do.

By late afternoon, the little apartment I shared with the other girls on our team was full. We moved a table into the living room and used the couches as seats for us and our guests. I don't remember everyone who showed up or what it was like eating around that table with the plush birthday hat someone had placed on my head.

What I remember was being in our tiny kitchen, with the windows cranked open as hot oil spluttered and the dumplings fried into crispy triangles. I folded the skins around ground beef mixed with garlic and sesame oil, tofu, and veggies, and showed the friends who braved the kitchen with me how to fold them too. I told them that these weren't exactly the right shape while sweat dripped down my face and behind my ears.

As we folded and sealed each dumpling with fingers dipped in water, then placed them into puddles of oil, I told them how my mom would make them, how my dad liked to dip them in Pace picante sauce, and how we always had more than one kind of sauce on the table. I told them how I would eat one after another, many of which were stuffed into my mouth by my mom, until my belly bloated and I felt like I might sink deep into the earth. And still I'd eat just one more.

What I remember most about my time in Germany is being so far from home yet feeling more at home with myself and the people in my life than I'd felt for years. I remember feeling like one barrier between God and me had been removed and I could accept his love in a way I'd never received it before.

I ended up living in Germany for three nonconsecutive years. I met Natalie, Kais, and Navina there, all of them mixed-race Germans who told me, in different ways, that they felt caught between worlds. As I look back on my meetings and friendships with each of them, I can see the way God used them to reach me, even when I was far away from myself and my own story.

With these friends, I shared stories about my family, and I listened as they shared their own. We talked about our mixed faces and what it felt like to bare them in various places and the ways we felt like we never really belonged in one place or another. I connected with them in this rare commonality, and I felt guilty that this connection was so grounding to me as a brand-new missionary—someone others would see as a "professional Christian."

I was astounded that those feelings of liminality are global. *Shouldn't spiritual connections alone be grounding for me?* I wondered. But here's what I realized during those years overseas, as I experienced feeling at home with these German friends: this part of me sorely needed a place to stretch its limbs and come out of hiding behind my fig leaves. It was in Germany that God showed me how far from home I truly was. This part of me needed to show up so that it, too, could experience the love of God.

It was this part of my identity that God was calling out to, asking again and again, "Where are you? Why are you still hiding?" Even in Germany, with people I never imagined meeting or befriending—some of whom I worked and prayed with, and some who didn't even know who Jesus was—God was calling out to me. Like David, there was nowhere I could go from his Spirit, no way I could flee the intention of his creation.

◆

For years when I was young, my mom took nightly baths, and I would join her. We would pile our thick, black hair on top of our heads, so strong and stiff it would shoot up like onion sprouts. We scrubbed each other's backs with neon-colored, nylon washcloths, as if we were scrubbing potato skins being prepped for dinner. While skin was set loose, we let our muscles and the details of our day unbind and she told me stories. It was another kind of womb, this safe spot, hidden from the rest of the day.

Bath time was one of the only times my mom was relaxed and slow-moving (minus the scrubbing). It was the closest thing to a mother-daughter heart-to-heart that I knew of. But at some point I stopped going into the bath with her. It probably happened after telling a friend that I took baths with my mom and getting a wide-eyed response in return. I would still join her in the bathroom and scrub her back when she asked me to, and then I'd sit on the floor outside the tub, fully clothed, wound tight with the awareness of how this practice would be perceived by my peers. I slowly learned to hide cultural traditions like this— moments of needed connection and storytelling, clues to the imago Dei in me—under a blanket of everyday clothing.

After her bath, my mom would step out of the water, her entire body dripping and beet red. She slathered herself with lotion, making sure to cover the vertical, X-marked scars from her belly button down, courtesy of my sister and me. Then, covered with the scent of gardenias, with a tightened brow and a pointed finger, she would remind me that it was imperative for a woman to take care of her body, and she told me to stop hiding mine.

The rest of that year in Germany, I occasionally perused Indian-German grocery stores, studying ingredients that were foreign to me yet brought me a little bit closer to home. I scrubbed our bathtub clean and soaked in it, asking my mom if she would send a care package that included a nylon washcloth.

It was in those baths of remembrance, and the stores that weren't quite the same as home but were close enough, that I began to understand the sacred and secular overlap. God is over all, and all belongs to God. If we pay close attention, we will find God everywhere, relentlessly pursuing each of us, speaking the truth in love through mandu skins and memories made and remembered in the womb of a tiny German kitchen.

When I left Germany after living there for two years, I vowed to return. Not only did I love serving, connecting, and ministering to students cross-culturally but I had also tasted the closeness of God and experienced a reawakened wonder at God's love as I rode fast-moving trains and walked cobblestone streets. Longings I'd forced into a deep sleep woke up again, groggy but present and persistent.

The international ministry I worked with in Germany was an ambitious, go-getting, evangelistic ministry—at least, that's how I would have described them then. While those eight years of my life, both as a student and as a staff member, were full of growth and learning, I also remember how most of my job description pushed me far from the way I was naturally wired and how I believed this was a good thing.

I forced myself to be more extroverted than I was, and I learned to interact in a more social and bubbly way "for the sake of the gospel." While I thought it was the right thing to do, it never felt quite right inside. I ignored that feeling because I believed it was evidence of my being wrong: too slow, too quiet, too contemplative, too doubtful, too soft—too Asian in ways that hindered me from using my body and my life as a living expression of the gospel.

During a team meeting one year, my teammates exchanged notes of encouragement, affirming the ways we saw God in one another. One of my teammates wrote, "You are a poetic thinker, and that is so rare in our ministry." Another teammate wrote, "You are introspective and insightful, and I've never met anyone who can see the connections of one's past showing up in their present like you do."

I knew these words from my teammates were true and intended to encourage me, but I was ashamed of them. No matter how hard I tried not to be who I was, no matter how hard I tried to guard the figurative front door of me, they could all see through me to find a deep thinker who felt most comfortable looking at the world through poetry and listening to other people's stories—hardly a know-it-all, go-getter evangelist with charm and charisma.

When we begin to see the interconnectedness of our search for identity and our search for Jesus, we will begin to head toward home and help others head toward home—and toward being truly known. We can't separate a person from their ethnic identity. The sentiment of killing the Indian, but keeping the child,[4] from North American boarding school days, is a colonial philosophy that has been passed on through generations of American history. A look back through history tells us how this violent story of assimilation—whether through force or by slow and subtle intention—is our story, and primarily a North American Christian story.

My own racial reckoning began with remembering. In snapshots and moments of realization, I was faced with past pain and my own choices to reject parts of my legacy. From trying to squelch my voice in cross-cultural ministry to dumping miyeokguk down the drain as a brand-new mom, I began to realize that I couldn't know God's love for me unless I accepted and uncovered all of who he has made me to be.

I had to go back to those moments of practicing my handwriting, moving to Indiana, rejecting my identity, deciding to no longer join my mom in the bath, and every other attempt to sew my own fig leaves in shame, and let God meet me in those places. Each memory is a wake-up call, a second chance that points me toward hope, wholeness, and healing.

These days when I feel lonely in my Asian American body or when the world feels too harsh and violent toward Asian American bodies, I intentionally go back to my memories. I remember the moments when I felt most at home. I remember what it felt like to sweat while frying mandu in an eighties-style German kitchen while the oil popped, interrupting our conversation.

I remember moments when shalom wasn't just something to long for but something that wrapped itself around me, reminding me this is the body God gave me, with a biracial Asian American heart, mind, and soul, where the Holy Spirit dwells. It was never meant to be a barrier to being whole and at home; it was through this exact vessel of veins and genes, through the precise distance between my eyes, and through every thick, textured hair on my head, that God intended for me to understand that I am known and that Immanuel is with me.

CHAPTER 8

HAN AND HOPE

There is no greater agony than bearing
an untold story inside of you.

MAYA ANGELOU

I scanned the large room, counting how many others there were like me. I saw next to none, and I began counting other women of color. It's a habit. On day one of the livestream IF:Gathering, I counted maybe five other women of color in the whole room.

I kept this number to myself; this habit helps me know how comfortable I'll likely be in a particular setting and how much I'll have to guard myself against what's consistently argued to be the good intentions of others.

I know, I know, I thought. *It's my job to keep this tension, to understand where everyone else is coming from at all times, to be extra grateful, and to remember that others can only know what they know.*

It all sounds good and right, as long as I ignore how I feel and make sure I never expect anyone else to do the same.

On the second day of the gathering, there was a Be the Bridge panel about race. A group of five or six women from diverse ethnic and cultural backgrounds sat at a table, sharing their experiences of racism and their own misunderstandings and pain.

I sat in the audience surrounded almost exclusively by white women. Most were listening intently. I noticed a stranger a few rows back roll her eyes. I listened to these women while looking for other women of color, wondering what they were feeling and experiencing. My body was shaking, and I couldn't stop it no matter how hard I tried.

The conversation was so close to home, but I'd never felt comfortable talking about this in any of the faith communities I'd been a part of. It felt like all the things I'd held inside for so long were raging within me, trying to break out of my skin.

After the gathering, I got a Facebook notification from the group of local participants. Tanorria posted about her desire to bring women together for a Unity Table—a gathering similar to the one we watched at the conference.

I immediately responded, "Yes!" I didn't need to think; my body had already decided for me.

A few weeks later, I was standing at the front door of an Indianapolis home holding a bottle of wine, trying to remember whose house this was.

I took a deep breath, and Tricia, the only woman not of color there, opened the door with a baby in her arms. The smell of fried chicken filled my nose. I heard laughter and voices emanating from the kitchen.

I walked in and placed the wine bottle on the island, where there were already enough sides to cover almost every square inch of space. Tanorria was checking on the chicken, and then she turned to face me and say hello.

She was one of the five other women of color I'd noticed at the gathering, and one of only two Black women I'd counted. A few seconds later, the doorbell rang, and the other Black woman from the event was standing at the door, smiling widely. Rebecca introduced herself and hugged me like Grandma Margie used to, without any air between us or a second thought about it.

That night we ate together, read Scripture, and

shared our first experiences of racism. I was floored to be sitting at a table where I'd been not only welcomed as a Korean American woman of faith but asked about my story. I didn't have to gauge everyone else's comfort level and decide if that was more important than what I had to share.

I didn't have to give qualifiers about how I knew the other person in my story probably had good intentions. I didn't have to attach clichéd endings to my story about how I'd forgiven and moved on because of my security in Jesus. No one told me I was being political or trendy. I didn't have to lighten the mood by making the experience into a joke.

I shared my story, and the women around the table were strong enough and soft enough to sit in the hurt with me. Their stories were different, but they understood the pain of my experience and the anguish of holding my stories in for so long.

My insides felt a little calmer than usual, and my guard came down one layer after another, while the other women in the room listened. It was the first time I'd been in an intentional gathering with other Christians where we talked about the intersection of our faith and our ethnic and cultural identities.

I looked at Melissa's black hair and listened to her talk about what it felt like to be a Chinese American woman at her church and workplace. I heard Rebecca share about leading others in worship as a Black woman. Tanorria shared her fried chicken with us, along with her dream to do more with cooking and diversity and inclusion. Tricia took everything in, caring for us, listening to our stories, and offering her whole heart and home at the same time.

God was using our stories to lead us, collectively, toward wholeness and home.

◆

After that night, I decided to write down some of the stories I'd begun sharing with others. I wrote about what it felt like to be spit on and poked by toothpicks or by questions. The more I wrote, the more it all kept coming, sloshing around and pouring out of my body as if I'd smashed stories into every open space inside me.

I wrote without concern about whether I was sharing the gospel in pretty paragraphs. I wrote honestly, reaching deep into the places where pages had been crumpled up and shoved into the corners. They'd never gone away; they hadn't disintegrated, despite all my rejection.

I went back to the stories I wrote in college, the ones I left behind over a decade earlier, when I was unsure how they fit into my life as a "professional Christian."

I found a little bit of healing with every sentence I scrabbled together on journal pages or pumped out on my computer screen.

Word by word, I filled journals, posted little essays on my blog, and wrote articles that I thought no one else would read. I started meeting with three other writer friends from church, and the more we talked about writing and shared words with one another, the more the stories spilled out of me.

I wrote one article on my blog that gained steam, and fellow church members began to respond. Sandy, one of the members of the writing group, who is biracial and Latina and also one of my closest friends, called me to say, "I read your article. What are you trying to do with it?"

I was taken aback by her words, realizing that up until now, we'd barely scratched the surface in our conversations about being biracial women of color.

I considered her question. What *was* I trying to do? More than any plan or agenda, it was as if the words and stories had a life of their own—they refused further silence. I couldn't settle for surface-level belonging anymore. The stories inside were out of control, like small children with too much sugar, and there was no way for me to force them to stay put or tidy any longer.

Sandy and I had been friends for a few years at this

point. We met when we were assigned as coleaders of a moms' group. I always took comfort in her dark hair and eyes, and in knowing she was biracial, but aside from sprinkles of conversation spurred by current events, our ethnic and cultural identities weren't major players in our connection.

She was there the summer after Ferguson, when my longing for depth in community shifted. I remember making eye contact with her during some of those small group discussions and prayer requests, and at the time, I thought they were looks of understanding.

I held the phone to my ear while staring out our dining room window, surprised to find that Sandy and I might not see eye to eye in our journey toward understanding our ethnic and cultural identities. I felt the need to defend my words, but as I responded that day, I sensed that I was actually defending both of us, no matter how varied our understanding and experience seemed to be.

We chatted for a few more minutes, and I considered whether my writing—and the way it rocked the boat— was worth it. As awkward as it was, this conversation shook open a new and needed can of worms between us. It slowly moved us toward connecting on a deeper level. We were in different places when it came to the rejection/embrace of our ethnic and cultural stories, but sharing a bit of our experience made room for us to see ourselves and each other in a new way.

Sharing our stories brings other people's stories into the light. Maybe you need to share your story with a big crowd, or maybe with just one other person. Maybe you will sing or scribble down poetry or raise your voice for justice in a way that challenges and creates opportunities for change. Maybe the sharing of your story will cause a jolting, uncomfortable response, or maybe the impact will be quiet and slow, an almost invisible awakening at work. No matter what it looks like, every story shared in love is an act of courage and kindness that will connect people and multiply good.

◆

Since that phone conversation, Sandy and I have walked together, reflecting back on our lives and looking ahead. When she told me a story about her grandpa Castillo, I knew we were in a sacred space. Today, when she shares her design and decor projects on Instagram, inviting people into her work of building like her ancestors did, intentionally using colors and patterns that reflect her multiethnic heritage, it's an online sermon of color and life.

I've shared bowls of bibimbap with her, and she has eaten more rice than her mostly grain-free stomach can handle. We've texted each other about a million "What are you?" encounters we've had with strangers and fellow churchgoers, exchanged book recommendations that give insight and color to our once-homogenous theology, and learned to laugh and cry together about being told (again and again) that we look exactly alike when we happen to be the only women of color in the room.

We've shared heartbreaks, grievances, and struggles. We have a friendship in which our differences are no longer avoided or in competition but embraced, and that has changed everything for both of us. Her flourishing as a Latina woman who loves Jesus and knows she's loved by Jesus brings me closer to flourishing in all God has made me to be.

As I spent time writing and putting my words and stories out into the world, I found more and more people with a story to tell. Our voices, however different, join together to remind us and others that we aren't alone. I discovered other writers online who have become my friends and have invited me into safe, supportive places. I learned that I can lean on these sisters across the miles, sending voice messages and notes like I used to exchange on Sanrio paper, folded and sent to California. We can lament across technology together, reminding one another who we are and who Jesus is, and rejoice with one another over our individual and communal stories.

———◆———

Five years ago, I gathered a diverse group of local women to speak on a panel for a group of moms at my church, sharing stories of racism, assimilation, and microaggressions. Before we walked onstage and shared our stories, we started a Facebook group so we could get to know each other.

As I read posts and messages from fellow Asian American and biracial women, from white women with spouses and/or kids of color, from Black women, Latina women, and recent immigrants, I soon realized that our connection might be even more important than sharing on the panel. These women of color expressed to me that for the first time, they felt comfortable talking freely about their stories. Many of them had never been asked. We had different backgrounds and upbringings, but we'd been mentored or discipled to assimilate and not rock the boat with our stories of pain and identity.

On the day of the event, I saw tears in the eyes of audience members. On one hand, seeing this gave me the reassurance that these fellow moms were listening and engaging with the stories, but in the back of my mind, I wondered if the tears would go any further than our time together. Were we just a movie that delivered a stir of emotions for a moment? But I also saw the way we shared the mic onstage, nodding at one another in solidarity, and how it emboldened all of us to find our voices and speak up. Every story we shared was a step home to ourselves.

Our ethnic and cultural identity isn't what saves us; only Jesus can do that. However, these gifts of ethnicity and culture are love letters from God. They are deliberate tools that reflect his love and intention. Through our curiosity and willingness to embrace these gifts, we can experience more of what Paul prayed for the Ephesians: "May you have the power to understand, as all God's people should, how wide, how long, how high, and how deep his love is."[1] The more we see and know how deep within us and how far beyond us God's love stretches, the more we understand how big God's love is for the world.

I recently started gathering a small group of Asian American women of faith who live in my area. It began out of my own desperation and disappointment. After years of going without other Asian American friends in my daily life, I began to wonder why we live where we do. I asked myself, *Are there really so few Asian Americans here?*

As I grew in motherhood, my longing grew for other

mothers who felt the burden of maintaining cultural values while encouraging their children to be their own people. When my oldest came home from kindergarten to tell me that his classmates had pulled the corners of their eyes at him, I wanted to tell other mom-friends who knew what it felt like to experience that very thing—both as a kid themselves and as a mother. When our second son told me that someone didn't believe he was Korean, and when we brought our youngest home from Korea and I watched her stop speaking Korean after the trauma of being adopted, I wanted to talk to other Asian American moms about the loss of heritage and how it leaves holes in us—and all the ways we try to fill these holes or fall into them.

I felt desperate to connect with other women who had Asian moms and were trying to navigate being moms as second- or third-generation Asian Americans. I wanted to know where they got their hair cut and if they had the same hair problems I did.

I cried out to God with these longings, asking him why we lived in a place with so few Asians. I remembered my camp friends who lived in large Asian American communities in Northern and Southern California, and I was sure their lives were more complete than mine. Was that the answer to everything? Did we need to move?

Shortly after this, I kept coming across Asian American women I knew, whether on my social media feed or in the grocery store. When I did, I could almost hear God say, *Here's one.*

Bit by bit, a handful of names and faces started stirring in my mind while I heated chicken broth to make soup for dinner or paddled out rice, freshly cooked in our rice cooker. I'd tell myself that these women were probably already content and didn't feel such a longing for other Asian American friends. Maybe it was just me and my ever-discontented Enneagram-four self who thought I was missing something everyone else had.

But their faces wouldn't leave my mind, and to this day I believe God was responding to the cries of my heart. I emailed these women and asked if they wanted to get together. I told them how I'd been longing for connection with other Asian American women, hoping they wouldn't think I was crazy or needy. Almost all of them responded with a resounding yes.

The first time we got together, there were only four of us, and some of us were meeting for the first time. We talked in the small back room of a local coffee shop for hours—about our families, our churches, our experiences as Asian American women navigating life in the Midwest. And suddenly, I wasn't so alone anymore. A connection line was drawn between our lives, and I was able to stretch out my questions, concerns, hopes, and experiences in a place where I didn't have to explain them or feel "othered" by them.

I left a little surer of who I was, a little more at home in my season of life, a little more aware of Jesus' presence in our Asian American details, and a little more comfortable with the reality of my pain.

Over the past five years, our group has continued to meet and grow. The core group of us represents seven local churches and a variety of backgrounds and expressions of the church. We've met in homes with small babies crawling around us, we've fed each other home-cooked meals and takeout, we've taken up big tables at brunch restaurants, we've met for tea, we've texted and prayed together, and we've invited more women into our togetherness.

Through the rise of visible anti-Asian sentiment during COVID-19, we clung to each other—all of us carrying both disappointment and hope. We were weary of being the ones who had to say something or remind people that the Asian American experience matters for more than us, but that it should matter even if it were only us.

On the day my daughter got into our van after school and told me that someone made fun of her kimchi and rice at lunch, I messaged my friends about it. One of the women in the group reached out to us after she was mocked while shopping for groceries at Walmart, and another told us about her son, who was spit at while running. Another friend shared about how recent events reminded her of her childhood, growing up as one of the only Asian and biracial Americans in her small Indiana town. She remembers being chased home from school by other classmates almost every day because her face and skin were different from everyone else's.

We messaged each other about our shared longing for our churches to acknowledge the violence against Asian Americans that was escalating during the pandemic—not just once, like it was an item on a to-do list. We talked about how we hadn't learned much about the history of Asian Americans in school and how there was no acknowledgment of Asian American contributions at all. We shared books and resources with each other, because we've learned to find these stories and tell them ourselves.

After the Atlanta massacre of Asian American spa workers in 2021, a core group of us started chatting more regularly on a video messaging app. We shared our hurts and frustrations, how our bodies shook, how we felt the weight of trauma and fear when we read the news in the weeks that followed. We understood what it was like to move, work, and be in our Asian American female bodies. This community was a safe space for our expressed anger, our feelings of rage, and our memories of being exoticized as Asian women.

It wasn't just the pain we felt from the amplified anti-Asian violence that made us desperate for one another; it was a combination of factors: the intergenerational trauma we carried, our love for Jesus, and the desire deep in our bones for belonging. We understood that human suffering and sadness attach themselves to the heart and the womb—han that is passed on from one generation to the next. We watched it unfold in our parents' lives as they did dishes, dressed us, fed us, and went to work. What I didn't realize about our shared han was what it could create when we joined together.

Over the years, knit together through the threads of stories and conversations and video messages, our collective han has forged a communal story of hope.

We met in my backyard in May of 2021 to celebrate Asian American Pacific Islander Heritage month. I put together little gift bags filled with Asian sheet masks and Pocky/Pepero sticks, happy to bring familiar things that I wouldn't have to explain. We ate and ate, and ate some more, sharing our food as we shared our lives.

I brought my rice cooker to the table outside, and we all filled our plates with Korean, Taiwanese, Chinese, and Filipino food, along with Kroger deli items and Italian food, while commiserating over the pain we'd been feeling for the past month—and more.

We cried and followed a liturgical prayer of lament that Ann found online. One of the women joined us for the first time after reaching out to Rachel in the mall bathroom just days before, desperate to connect with another Asian American woman. She came and shared about her own search for faith, and I watched her weep with a plate of Asian food on her lap, talking about God and about being Chinese. In that moment, I realized we were experiencing church right there, eating together under the branches of my maple trees.

I've since learned that tigers rarely roar in the loud, ferocious way we assume they do. They are depicted as wild, isolated, exotic animals, but this is not their default state. Though their roaring is loud enough to paralyze other animals, they rarely do so.[2]

Tigers can communicate in a number of ways, and the sound of their communication is often carried at such a low frequency—called infrasound—that humans can't even hear it. In her study of biology and sound, bioacoustician Elizabeth von Muggenthaler found that though this infrasound can't be heard, it can be felt. The sound travels long distances and reaches past obstacles such as buildings, thick forests, and even mountains.[3]

I think about the invisibility that so many Asian Americans have carried throughout our nation's history, including these sisters and me.

I look around the circle in my backyard. Despite so much pain and loss, our voices aren't gone. We aren't alone; we uniquely embody a combined story of han and hope that's meant to connect us to others—both those who are like us and those who are unlike us. Our stories are built into our nation's railroads, restaurants, libraries, schools, streets, and foundations of faith.

We are writing them down, shouting them out in song and public outcries, the way only we can. Every time we come together, whether for picnics or protests, we have immense power to cultivate hope and rebuild our stories while supporting the stories of our brothers and sisters. There is a sound that reaches through the wilderness of invisibility, stretches across intergenerational trauma, and breaks down lies of assimilation and racial hierarchy to tell the truth and lay a new foundation.

It is the sound of our collective han and our connected hope.

CHAPTER 9

GHOSTS AND GLORY

One need not be a chamber to be haunted,
One need not be a house;
The brain has corridors surpassing
Material place.

EMILY DICKINSON

We weren't allowed to whistle in the house when I was growing up.

"YAAA!" my mom would scream the minute a tune began to escape from my lips.

"Sorry, I forgot," I'd say. It felt strange that my instinctive habit reminded her of nightmares.

"The bad men were whistling at me before everything. That's all I see when I hear the whistling."

I imagine the scene: the concrete wall these older

Korean men walked against, audacious and unafraid to let her know they were there, following her as if she were prey. But she was only a girl.

Before I had a name for things like oppression, imperialism, systemic racism, colorism, misogyny, and greed, I understood the way those ghosts haunted girls, families, and nations.

When my parents turned out the light at night, it wasn't just the darkness in my room I was afraid of; it was those things I couldn't name. It was the fear that these ghosts would inevitably come for me, the way they'd come for my mom before me, and hers before that. I was afraid of losing whatever semblance of safety and light I'd held on to during the day and having to surrender it all to the night and the unknown lurking behind the doors of tomorrow.

Whatever privilege I carried, I knew it could be stripped away in an instant if the ghost stories got out.

The mountainside cemetery was where everything went black. They brought her to a place of the dead. She says she woke up after someone yanked her hair, but the whistling men were gone. She had dirt in her fingernails and the scent of those men on her skin. Her shivering body was uncovered.

She was alone, and the ghost of the grave she lay upon had woken her, she told me. I wanted to tell her she was probably dreaming, and I wanted to know what the ghost looked like. Teetering between belief and disbelief, I studied her face and the lines around her eyes. She said she ran home and got in trouble with her aunt for being out so late. Her aunt saw her dirty, disheveled dress, but no one believed her.

Every time I heard the story, I held my breath, no matter how many times she'd told me.

My mom's life came unraveled because that's what war does. Life begins and life is taken in the aftermath of so much destruction. The news headlines said the war was over, but for my mom, it had just begun.

After the night in the cemetery, her relationship with her aunt grew worse. My mom was angry that her brother was in an orphanage and that no one believed what had happened to her. Not long after that, she ran away.

I would ask her, "What did you do? How did you survive after you ran away?" I tried to picture her running from these whistling ghosts, going from one lonely spot to another, washing dishes here, reaching for scraps there, and still running . . . running all the way to America.

By the end of grade school, I was afraid those whistling men were around every lonely alleyway. As I got older, I feared them in my school hallways. I met them when a high school athlete told me all the guys on his team were taking bets on whether one of their teammates could win me over—that I was the first girl to say no to him. He said they were tired of the girls who all looked the same—as if that should feel like a compliment to someone "exotic" like me. I wished I could set ghosts loose on them in their locker room.

In college, I found these men in the counseling session when the counselor rubbed my back for a little too long, and I got up and left before the appointment was done. No one believed me when I said I knew it wasn't just an encouraging pat on the back, and no one questioned why a school counselor would be patting a student on the back, either. What would it take for someone to believe me? Why is it so hard for people who say they've received Jesus as their Savior to believe how ugly sin can be—or that it's crafty enough to corrupt entire systems?

Everyone wants proof of our ghost stories, but they forget that it's women like me—little sisters, moms with accents, grandmothers at the grocery store, women working at a spa in Atlanta—who are chased by ghost stories like these. And beyond the subjugation of women, the fetishizing of Asian women in particular is an added braid of racism that has an impact for generations.

When I first met Matt, I was relieved to find out that he didn't have a "thing for Asians." It meant there was a chance he could see me as a real person, quirks and all—a biracial Korean American woman with a multicultural upbringing—and embrace whatever that meant to me and what it would mean over time. It's taken years of us being together for me to believe that I can trust this is true.

◆

I found the traditional Korean folktale "Kongji and Patji" in an empty hotel gift shop in Seoul one summer. Soft elevator music played while I reached for the book with my sticky seven-year-old fingers. My mom nudged my dad as I held it, then she nodded her head toward the cash register. He bought the book.

I read and reread the legend of Kongji. I studied the illustrations and paid close attention to the faces of each of the Korean girls, wondering if I resembled them. I wanted to tie my hair in a tight bun at the nape of my neck, but I had no hair around my neck to gather. I regretted the poofy-topped pixie haircut I'd begged my mom to get a few weeks before our trip. I thought I looked like a boy instead of a beautiful Korean girl.

I said their names in my head over and over again: *Kongji, Patji. Kongji, Patji.* I looked in the mirror and saw the summer freckles that had shown up across the bridge of my nose and wondered if that's what the author meant when describing the "pockmarks" across Patji's face—one of the descriptions of the "mean girl" of the story. It would be years before I said this out loud or knew how to articulate it, but I wondered, *Am I bad because I'm biracial? And if so, which side of me is the ugly side? Which part of my ethnic heritage represents Patji, and which one represents Kongji?*

I knew this Korean version of the Cinderella story before I discovered the Disney movie and became distracted by lovable Gus, the glass slippers, the pumpkins, and the dream that love could find a woman hidden behind layers of grief, poverty, abuse, and her own wild imagination. But every time I tried to put myself in Cinderella's slippers, I remembered my unruly, textured, mixed-race hair and the marks on my face and the way my nose and eyes were just a bit left of center. I remembered all these details until I was sure that this story, like every other story I'd heard, wasn't intended for me.

I carried my ache to belong around with me like an extra bag attached somewhere between my heart and hips. I felt it when I read stories, when I walked busy city streets, when I listened to my parents argue, and when I played alone, tired of the sound of my own voice.

Kongji is praised for her selfless servanthood. She's naturally beautiful, without any effort, and she always does the right thing. She is pure to the end and has no need for forgiveness or grace. The folktale, centuries old, was passed down orally from the time of the Joseon Dynasty. It reaches further than the Disney story, creating a narrative about good and evil, help and judgment, dreams coming true and the death of dreams.

In a way, this story taught countless Koreans that keeping your head down, working hard, and being selfless and good would mean all your dreams could come true. There are echoes of this narrative carrying into the Korean diaspora as the Asian American immigrant story merges with the American Dream. Kongji seems like the model of all good things—and the way to good things coming true.

But as the story of Asian America goes, when we arrived as Kongji, whether on shore, at an airplane gate, or as a second or third generation, America called us foreign and fetishized us. America wanted to both save us and send us back to where we came from. America wanted to lead us, then demonize us—to subdue us and stand on our backs to build the American dream.

The photograph celebrating the completion of the Transcontinental Railroad is forever seared in my mind. I was watching the PBS five-hour film series called *Asian*

Americans.[1] Despite the fact that the railroad builders included twenty thousand Chinese immigrants, they were originally cropped out of the photo that commemorated the event. Just over a decade after the completion of the railroad, President Chester A. Arthur signed the Chinese Exclusion Act, which banned immigration of Chinese laborers.

This isn't just ancient history, either. In the last few years, with social media posts blaming China and, in some cases, all Asians for bringing COVID-19 to our nation, our faces and families have been renamed as a virus: the infection of a nation.

In the end, it's Kongji's ghost that redeems her name and finds justice, but the story leaves her floating through liminal space and time, destined to be a wispy version of her embodied self—forever alone.

When you don't fit into the history of any part of your heritage, you begin to wonder if you truly are a ghost.

I wonder who pulled my mom's hair to wake her to her dark reality. Who urged her out of that cold cemetery to face the rest of her life?

God saw and knew the ghosts of Hagar's story, and through her, he wrote a new one. As an Egyptian slave of Abraham and Sarah (Abram and Sarai at the time), Hagar was given to Abraham so she could bear a child for him when Sarah could not. Hagar's life was irrevocably altered as Sarah made decisions based on her doubt. She no longer believed God would come through on his promise to her and her husband—that they would bear children, and many of them.

Hagar carried the weight of Sarah's doubt, literally and figuratively. When she became pregnant, Sarah resented her, and the relational tension between them became a burden too great to bear. So, like my mom, Hagar ran away. But God found her in the wilderness.

Hagar and Abraham's son, Ishmael, would be a reminder to her and to all who listened to her story that God hears our cries and the cries of those we love. Her experience with God in the wilderness showed her that God saw not only the world but also the details of her story. This intimate moment with God, in the middle of her worst nightmare coming true, gave her confidence in his goodness and his love for her. She responded and called him by name: *El-roi*.[2]

Hagar is the first and only person in the Bible to name God like this. Think about what she might have been led to believe about the God of Abraham and Sarah prior to this experience. As an Egyptian, she likely didn't know or believe in the Hebrew God that they worshiped. Maybe she prayed to other gods or doubted a higher power existed at all. And yet God found her, letting her experience his expansive love.

God is actively looking for the ones that his people usually overlook. The church will not stay confined to the walls we try to keep it in. This should change the way we see and pursue people; it should change the way we minister and the way we love our neighbors. There's movement toward the Kingdom of God in places we'd never expect, and it begins with stories in desert places and cemeteries, stories about nightmares and ghosts. God is not afraid of the one who is thirsty, the one who runs away, the foreigner, the betrayed, the lonely, the battered, and the fearful.

God's love stories start with people like these.

I think of the nights as a child when I heard my mom say she didn't want to live anymore—the nights my dad held her, both of them crying, as he kept her from hurting herself. I think of the ghost stories that haunted her and the ones that must have haunted Hagar, wherever her life ended up after the day she met God in the desert and called him a new name.

I go back to my mom's ghost stories often. From mothers and grandmothers and great-grandmothers before her, these ghosts have crossed oceans and survived generations. Their stories stay with me, like scars I can't erase. If we don't learn to see Jesus in our ghost stories and scars, how will we know him or believe he knows us?

Embracing our stories isn't about adding flair to a three-minute testimony of salvation. There's nothing wrong with capturing the short version of things, but telling those stories merely as a means to an end discredits our witness as believers. The brief testimonies I've heard mattered to me for a moment, but when I witness people embracing the entirety of their stories (and when I embrace my own), it sustains my faith for the long haul. As I listen to stories that are still unfolding, even the ones told with anxiety shaking the lips of the teller, I experience the love of Jesus in and through those I wouldn't have expected it from.

My mom said she used to dream about Jesus. As in her recurring tiger dream, she dreamed she was looking at the back of Jesus' head, reaching for his shoulders, begging him to turn around so she could see his face. She spoke of the dream with such desire and reverence, and in those short moments, I understood the gospel in a way no one could tell me through mini booklets, pat answers, or the forced rehearsal of a testimony.

I always thought I was supposed to get rid of ghost stories—to throw them out with my childhood stack of R. L. Stine books, or to smash them and burn them, and then to sing victorious worship songs afterward, finally free. But that never worked for me. While the books were gone, the haunted feeling kept coming back, no matter how hard I tried to hide it. The problem with having to throw things out or burn them is that this kind of removal doesn't require the Savior. Jesus becomes a prop, and we act as our own saviors, trusting our own ability to rid ourselves of fear and sin, when it has never been in our power to do so.

Instead, I sit with Jesus in these ghost stories, with my fear out in the open. This has helped me to see and hold out hope for the kind of glory that can withstand the weight of my fears, darkness, and longing. Only Jesus can bridge the gap between our nightmares and our dreams.

Korean diasporic sons and daughters, mothers and fathers—those who are immigrants, multiracial, adoptees, first generation (or second or third)—are strangers in a strange land, like Hagar and Moses. Our ghost stories have sought to haunt us into silence and send us into isolation, but God has made it possible to bend those stories and shape them until they bear witness to his good glory.

◆

On our second trip to Korea as a family, my mom reunited with her baby brother. The first thing I noticed was their hair. They had the same thick, coarse strands—so strong you could floss with them. They embraced and wept, and though I'd never seen him before, I knew we were connected.

Walking the streets of Busan, my mom skipped with him, arm in arm. They shared an umbrella and fed each other banchan at mealtimes. They laughed until they cried, and cried until they laughed and held hands like children. Watching them showed me that birth culture and family matter in a way I'd never grasped before.

I clung to my uncle's big smile, watching his every move, hoping his loud laugh would erase some of the ghosts with the glory of reunion, reconciliation, and redemption.

Near the end of our trip, my mom and I visited a famous park full of sculptures a few blocks from our hotel. Every inch of my body was sticky from the July heat. I heard cicadas buzzing and buses humming, and the sun shone through the tree leaves overhead. I couldn't wait to get back to the hotel to swim, eat kimchi, and get a drink of water.

Suddenly, something cold pelted my head and then my bare arm. Bird poop. My mom started laughing hysterically as I stood frozen on the sidewalk like a one-armed scarecrow. She howled something about how this was good luck. "It must be a fat one—so much poop!"

We didn't have anything to wipe it off with except a small handkerchief my mom found in her purse. She wiped at it and then bent over laughing, wiped, then laughed again—on and on she went like this, while the rest of Seoul walked around us, pretending not to notice us or the predicament we were in: Korean mother, mixed daughter, and Korean bird poop.

Our hands were too full to fan our laughter away, and it grew like a flame gone wild. We walked back to the hotel arm in arm, me with my messy right arm extended and white bird poop smeared across it, my mom with the now-nasty handkerchief in her hand, and both of us laughing the whole way.

There were memories like this one, when I felt just right—overtaken by an otherworldly sense of belonging. We laughed in the face of being on the margin and standing out. We refused to stay quiet about who we were, not caring if our togetherness as mother and daughter was being questioned. My mother's wide-mouthed laughter left no room for thought about whether there was food stuck in her teeth or about joyful tears being squeezed out of the corners of her eyes or about stopping mid-step to bend over howling.

When we laughed together like this, I felt the hope of shalom. I thought of her laughing this way with her baby brother after decades apart. I began to believe things could be made right in my mom's irreconcilable stories—and my own. Our ghost stories were being smoothed and reshaped with love and laughter.

On the streets once described as haunted, the glory of God was evident and present, writing new pages.

JESUS AND JEONG

History has failed us, but no matter.

MIN JIN LEE

When my mom arrived in the United States for the first time at twenty years old, officials misspelled her name and changed her birth date. To this day, we don't know if she was born in March or December. What we know is that she was born during a time in Korea when one third of the population was homeless. Her country was divided in two by people who weren't Korean and yet claimed some type of ownership there nonetheless.

She was born in a country that was being shaken awake from the nightmares of Japanese colonization and war. The result wasn't just a peninsula split in two; families were permanently divided and people were erased. Their photos and memories were burned up or discarded, parents were taken away from their children, and new division lines were made that could not be crossed. I was two years old when she became a US citizen, and instead of keeping the botched name she was given upon arrival, she chose her own name: Jeong.

Jeong is a Korean word that has no accurate English translation. Like my story, this word contains multitudes. Jeong means love in the simplest sense, but it also encompasses many facets of love at the same time. Like Jesus' love, it's simple yet beyond simple logic, explanation, and limit. It's a feeling, a connection, an others-centered motivation for all things big and small.

Before I understood the significance of this Korean word, I sensed how my mom's name, whether it was written by my mother in Korean, English, and Japanese or spoken tenderly by my father, encompassed my mother's story—and how it now fills my own.

I felt jeong in every gigantic ssambap ball she stuffed into my mouth, every kimbap piece she handed me while she was rolling and preparing it for my sister and me, all while making enough to feed an entire neighborhood. I felt it in every back scrub, each story shared, every hair brushed so tightly my skin would lift toward my hairline. I felt it in each cucumber coin put on my face and every word of "San Toki" sung to me before I fell asleep at night.

Like Jesus, jeong has always been there, reaching for me, even when I rejected it and had no words to describe it.

———◆———

He looked up at me from his toddler bed and asked, "Can you sing me the song about the rabbit who runs away?"

I pulled the thin Pikachu sheet up around his small shoulders and sang "San Toki" while he made bunny ears and moved them up and down the length of his forearm.

"Why did the rabbit go away?" he asked.

I looked into his big brown eyes and saw myself staring back. They were filled with questions.

"I don't know," I said. "Maybe the rabbit wanted to see what was on the other side of the mountain. Maybe the little rabbit didn't believe it had enough at home."

I thought he was content to think about those possibilities, but after I kissed his forehead goodnight, he had more to say.

"I don't even like to go to school. If I was the rabbit, I would just stay home." The weight of his anxiety hung on his words, passing from his heart to my own. I wished I could take all of it away. "Who taught Halmoni that song?"

"I don't know—I guess it was her mommy." I lifted my arms over my head, making a saranghae circle, whispering a breath prayer for help before turning out the light.

I considered how little I knew about the lullaby and how I'd need to talk to Korean friends or do some research to understand more. I'd asked my mom about it in the past, but she didn't know anything beyond the song itself.

I wondered what kinds of cultural traditions and details my own kids would discover as they got older. Would they remember these things as treasures or an inheritance, passed on through generations of pain? Would they become embarrassed by such stories? Would they see themselves like the mountain rabbit, wandering far away from everything they'd come to know as home?

When I began to realize that Jesus is the Son of God and someone who would sit with me in the home of my upbringing, sharing the dried squid my mom roasted while sitting in a kimchi squat in front of our suburban Midwestern fireplace, it changed everything for me. I could look back and see him crying with me after I dropped that Korean class in college, depressed and confused by the unreachable words and sounds I never owned and by the generations of loss I didn't understand.

He wouldn't have poked me with a toothpick or spit on my sister and me while walking along the beach in Busan. He wouldn't have thought less of me for being mixed race; after all, according to Matthew's meticulous genealogy, Jesus was culturally Jewish, but his ancestors also included a Moabite (Ruth) and a Canaanite (Rahab).[1] Jesus' family tree was populated by ethnic groups that didn't get along and lived divided from one another.

Knowing this, I had to believe he would chuckle with me at my very Dutch maiden name and the irony of my deep love for all things potato—and call the whole of me good. He understands what it's like to come from people groups that avoid those of mixed race, whether by shame or law. He knows what it's like to come from broken and blended families. He knows what it's like to bear ethnic and cultural bridges in his body.

As these Spirit-led, grace-filled realizations sank in, I felt myself drowning in a sea of limitless love. I began to understand how my curiosity about and embrace of my heritage, my ethnicity, my story, and my cultural upbringing move me closer to Jesus. By accepting my ethnic and cultural identity with grace and patience, I am learning to understand my own belovedness and grow in my love for others.

This journey from rejection to embrace is an answer to Paul's prayer for the Ephesians—that they would be able to understand how wide and long and high and deep the love of Christ is. I wish the realizations had come much sooner. I wish the road to understanding weren't so long and lonely. I wish I had known that small things would lead me back home, from lullabies to soup bowls, from journal pages to the sharing of stories in safe communities, near and far. Then again, I'm not sure I would have known any of it in the same way without walking the journey in its entirety. And if bearing the burden of my own mistakes, pain, and hiding, and coming to understand that Jesus' perfect jeong is the only way out of it, helps others come home to him and themselves too, then may it all be so.

I couldn't embrace the good news of the gospel or the hope of Jesus' Kingdom come, here and now, until I embraced the good news written in my thick mixed hair, the face of Jesus' Kingdom staring back at me in the mirror. I had to learn not only that he didn't mind my kimchi-breath prayers but that if he were here with me in the flesh, he would have kimchi breath too.

I couldn't embrace the strength of true community,

koinonia, until I understood that Jesus meant for us to belong together by seeing one another, sharing and receiving one another's stories, pursuing one another, learning to love one another, and laying down our lives for one another as whole beings who carry stories of inherent value.

To know greater depths and widths of Jesus' love for me, I had to embrace the jeong that has permeated every page of my life since before I had breath—the jeong that compelled me to journey from rejection to embrace and to a redeemed curiosity that has led me to a life of building and rebuilding my family's ethnic and cultural stories.

In the book of Nehemiah, what stands out most to me is how tenderhearted Nehemiah remained toward his people and his ancestors, even though he was removed from them. Though he was in a culture different from his own, he had a sense of ethnic and cultural identity that was interwoven with his spiritual identity. He was familiar with Babylon and Babylonian ways, and he succeeded there, despite being born in exile, as a son of refugees.

I wonder what stories his family told him while he was growing up in Persia, away from the land of his ancestors. I wonder if some of these stories kept his heart tender toward home and helped him remember who he was, who his people were, and what God had done among them. Were these stories also what fueled his compassionate leadership despite opposition?

As he sought to rebuild the walls of Jerusalem and as he led his people in this work, he encountered both support and opposition. The support urged him on, and though he remained steadfast in his work, the opposition impacted him. He prayed with emotion over the constant accusations and interruptions. When others claimed he was rebuilding for personal gain or power, he responded by calling out what was false and staying steady in his work.

I've never built a wall, but I can relate to having to defend myself against naysayers. When I was in college, I mentioned something to a friend about how important my Koreanness was to me. She responded with her own paraphrased verses about how everything outside our identity in Christ will be burned up one day. Another friend told me that she didn't talk about her race or ethnicity unless she wanted attention, as if I'd just shared part of my story for that reason. I've been told that stories like mine are a trend, as if my entire upbringing and all the stories that make it are as light and meaningless as a leaf blowing in the wind.

Once, when I asked a church leader if diversity was a value in their ministry, I was told, "Yes, but many

people are weary from conversations about the impor-
tance of diversity."

All I could think about was how bone weary my
friends of color and I have been for years over the lack
of priority given to diversity. Why is it okay for us to
be weary but not okay for white brothers and sisters in
the faith?

I've also hidden my stories out of fear. I've covered
them up, tried to erase them, and spent years wishing
they weren't my own. I've resisted my tastebuds and
my cravings, I've tuned out the songs of my upbringing, and I've pretended I didn't need the flavors and
sounds that God chose to sustain me with in my mother's womb. I've told myself I could have a heritage and
let it all go and still be whole and free. I've believed the
lie of assimilation and white supremacy until it led me
to a dead end. I couldn't grow or be known by assimi-
lating. I couldn't experience being loved when part of
me was pushed aside. The isolation I experienced from
putting to death the details God intentionally placed in
me eventually broke me.

When I look closely and lean hard into the God-
given jeong that now compels me, I see Jesus doesn't
require me to throw out my cultural identity; rather,
he beckons me to rebuild my cultural stories on a
foundation of his perfect love. This rebuilding is not

self-serving work; rather, it creates refuge and room for my stories to flourish in God's love and good intention.

———◆———

Last year, my oldest son asked, unprompted by me, if we were having tteokguk for Lunar New Year. After hearing his question, all my kids exclaimed over how much they loved the soup. My son told his siblings that they would become a year older after eating the bright white rice cake coins, and I chuckled because I couldn't remember when I told them that or when they all decided tteokguk was their tradition to own—especially after their lackluster response the first time I made it.

Since we were talking about rice cakes, my youngest started begging to make our own songpyeon for Chuseok next year. She has the recipe dog-eared in her *Korean Celebrations* book. My middle child told Matt and me that he wants to take Korean classes, and when I listen to my Korean language lessons in the car, he eagerly follows along, repeating each of the words and phrases, so sure of his Koreanness despite his fair hair and light eyes.

I look in their faces and hear their questions and see how natural it is for them to want to know who they are and to reach deeper into their ethnic and cultural identity. This isn't something political or trendy for them. They have no agenda; there is no argument. They aren't looking for something to worship or idolize above their Maker. They search for language, stories, tastes, songs, and other creative expressions to connect with one another, with our family story, and with those who came before them. They are living evidence that representation matters, because it's a road map to knowing they are made whole by a Creator who loves every part of them.

They read books about the Loch Ness monster and ask my husband again what his Scottish crest looks like. They want to know when we will visit Korea so they can taste and see who they are in a way they haven't before. They want to see pictures of the Highlands in Scotland and look at our family tree online. Our youngest, who is adopted, wants to see the photo books made by her foster umma in Korea and the pictures of her earliest days—there and here. She wants to talk about where she was born and look at the city on the map. She told us she misses her biological mom, even though she doesn't know who she is. It's good and natural and affirming for my children to know who they are deep down, into their every detail. Their curiosity is holy, and to withhold this information from them would be wrong, because these details lead them to Jesus.

God speaks to me in English, but in my dreams he

sings to me in Korean. We are not only pilgrims; we are kajok, family. We are connected by jeong, rebuilding the bridges that have been broken down before us. God uses all of it to lead us toward wholeness and home.

———◆———

On the plane ride to bring our daughter home from Korea six years ago, we flew Korean Air. The flight attendant brought us a tray of bibimbap, and I excitedly squeezed my toothpaste-like tube of gochujang onto my rice mixed with vegetables. I noticed another container with the lid lifted to release steam. The steam seeped out of the opening, swirling toward me—an invitation of strength and grace. I watched it and felt the weight of being in between cultures, literally flying in airspace between the East and the West, reaching back toward Korea no matter how far I've been thrust away from it.

I am like Moses, just like my grandpa Dallas said I would be.

I am a daughter of Jeong, just like Jesus knew I would be.

I am Hagar, a stranger in the wilderness planting hope with tears of han—and I have a God who comes near.

I am another Nehemiah—a Korean mother who builds and rebuilds.

I pulled back the lid and saw the dark pieces of seaweed floating in the liquid and realized it was miyeokguk. I looked around to see if others had it on their trays and whether they'd eaten theirs. The woman in the row to the right of me moved her perfectly round spoon with a clump of rice on top toward the bowl of soup and dipped it in, adding broth and seaweed to her spoonful. It seems just like Koreans, that even on an airplane, they would offer their most comforting and traditional tastes.

I remembered how I poured a whole homemade pot of miyeokguk and a part of myself down the drain. I thought of all the things I'd rejected and all the things I'd hidden, and silent tears slid down my dried-out face.

I pulled the plastic lid all the way off, and though I knew I should use a spoon to be polite, I lifted the bowl and drank the entire contents, letting it gush down and caress my tongue, my throat, and eventually the insides of my midsection with forgiveness. It was a baptism of what I once was, a rebirth from rejection to the redemption of embrace. With each trembling swallow, I nourished the imago Dei within me.

———◆———

I recently found an English translation of "San Toki" online. I mouthed the words and sang it slowly in

Korean, then read the English translation. All these years I thought the story was about the rabbit getting lost and eventually finding its way back home. But I discovered the rabbit didn't exactly run away; it left to climb the mountain and find chestnuts to bring back home to its family. Perhaps my mom told the story that way to mirror her own journey. The idea that the rabbit went away, came back home, and also had chestnuts to feed its family fills me with new hope.

Mountain bunny, bunny
Where are you going?
Hopping, hopping while running,
Where are you going?

Over the mountain pass, pass,
I will climb it alone.
Plump, plump chestnuts
I'll find and bring some home.

The stories we've been told inform us, but we are also writing new stories to give away. I tell my kids about their halmoni's name, how it's a Korean word that means more than a thousand words. It's a word that describes the connection between their ancestors' dreams and their own unfolding stories. In between their bickering over who has the best seat at the table and who gets to pick what's for dessert, I tell them that they have jeong in their hearts, a voice they cannot hear but will always feel—something Jesus put there to help them understand how deeply they are loved and how all of us belong to one another.

I whispered the words of the song again, thinking about how one story always begins with two.

San-toki, toki-ya
Oh-di-rule gah-nun-yah?
Kkang-choong, kkang-choong di-myun-suh
Oh-di-rule gah-neun-yah?

San-gogae gogae-rule
Na honja noh-moh-soh
Toshil-toshil al-ba-mule
Ju-woh-soh wol-tay-yah.

Over time, as I've sung this lullaby to one child and then another, I've come to realize I am no longer voiceless. I have spent years far from home, and the journey back isn't quick or easy. The journey is ongoing, and it's mine to own, just as it will be for my children. I've gathered stories connected by jeong across oceans and generations and cultures. These stories are like chestnuts to feed and nurture other pilgrims in hiding, shalomsick travelers who need them to build and rebuild their own journey home.

As I sit on the couch with my kids, I point at the Korean picture books sent by my parents or the ones I've found online, trying to pronounce the Korean words I know. I watch their eyes and mouths move alongside mine. I know they feel the connection just like I did, however clumsy the words sound coming out of our mouths. I see the familiar desire to belong and be known as a part of family culture and identity.

I gather my stories alongside all the answers I don't know and offer them anyway: my own precious scraps of treasure. My heritage. I continue to reach back so I can reach forward and pass on the power of holy curiosity, despite so many things I still haven't figured out. I pray my children will take these pieces, fill their imaginations, and keep rebuilding what's been stolen and destroyed over generations—in a way only they can.

I can't offer every Korean dream or story, and I can't give them a voice of fluency, but I can offer them the example of holy curiosity at work. I can offer them what it looks like to daily embrace the imago Dei in my mixed biracial skin as I try again and again to make my own kimchi. I can let them see my frustration and my persistence as I practice language lessons while driving the car.

I can let them see where my limits have been set too narrowly, whether as a result of my own rejection or because of the loss I was born with, and trust God to widen those boundaries before their eyes. I can reach toward the redemption of my story and my parents' stories, and bring my children with me in my losses and my growth.

I can hold up my broken branches, with the pages of stories stapled to them like leaves, and stretch the arms of my own broken body out wide to make the shape of our family tree.

I am a beloved woman of jeong: a wandering tiger, a daughter and a mother. I am learning to speak the language of starlight: shouts of shalom into the threshold between the darkness and the light.

SILLA AND GOCHU: A FOLKTALE

A fictional story inspired by my family's stories, past and present, and told to my daughter during bathtime

Tell me what it means
When a tiger roars
And no one hears.

Tell me how a bird builds a nest
When she's a magpie
Who forgot how to sing.

Is there a place for us,
Can you find us,
Did you make us
In the silence
Of our mother's wombs?

Will you redeem
These stories
From nightmares and tombs?

Once upon a time, there was a city girl who became a poet and fought wars with her words. She married the son of farmers. Her husband was an archer who grew up in the mountains and knew how to talk to animals. But their story begins with another story, as all stories do.

Once upon a time, there was a magpie named Silla who lived in the thin branches of a hibiscus tree in the city.

Silla did her morning sweep through the city, flying low to listen to friends and enemies, coworkers and neighbors, schoolchildren and their pets chatter about the details of their days. She kept a mental list, connecting their activities silently in her head.

The conversations were the same as they'd been for a thousand years, recorded in the songs passed down from one generation of magpies to the next.

Silla listened to the songs of her mother and father, but she refused to sing. She learned to write with a pen she found in someone's backyard, along with a measure of persistence her parents always said came from a power beyond them.

She found the pen glimmering under a wooden tree swing one day when she was making her rounds. The pen's translucent middle caught her eye as it flashed yellow in the bright spring light. She carried it away in her black beak.

She always showed her treasures to Gochu, the tiger—her best and biggest friend.

Silla and Gochu liked to compare their markings. Gochu said that Silla looked like a small penguin that could fly, and Silla liked to say that Gochu looked like gochugaru gone bad, with a black river of ants running through it—drunk and dizzy from the spice.

They didn't know what drew them together, despite how many things should have pulled them apart. Silla knew other magpies who had become breakfast or a midnight snack on account of being near a tiger at the wrong time. And Gochu knew that most magpies flew to places where a tiger's strength and growl could never reach, singing prideful songs about their craftiness and riches. He knew more than one tiger who had been tricked by the cunning mind of a magpie.

Nevertheless, these two unlikely friends regularly sat near the hibiscus with the pink and white blooms. Silla sat in the tree and Gochu lay in its shade, and they had long conversations about the problems in the world and the beautiful things they found in it.

Every day, they wondered how to solve these problems and keep the beautiful things from fading away.

Their unusual friendship isolated them from other magpies and tigers that couldn't understand how they ever agreed on anything or what they did with their disagreements.

Silla insisted, "Gochu sees the world in a different way, and I wouldn't notice that perspective if I didn't listen to him."

Silla's eonni said their nests were more important than seeing the world through other eyes, especially scary glowing eyes like a tiger's. She was convinced Gochu could not be trusted and regularly watched out for her little sister while shaking her beak at her poor choices.

Gochu's friends didn't understand why he would stay awake and use his afternoons for long, boring conversations with a bird. They assumed Gochu had a sneaky plan up his sleeve and was using Silla to capture all the magpies in the city for lunch. They observed him with a watchful eye, waiting to prove that Gochu was a yamche—sneaky and selfish, not merely crazy enough to befriend a bird to chat with under the flowers.

There was a family of garlic farmers on the mountainside near Gochu's home. He was afraid of the father and mother, who were known to use their perfect aim and quick bow-and-arrow skills to take care of anything that threatened their home or family. But Gochu had watched these mountain farmers care for their children and tend to the earth with such kindness and care that he couldn't help but try to keep them safe.

At dusk each day, the father took a break from his work and brought his son and daughter out for archery practice. The mother had made a target from an old piece of cloth and filled it with rice. Gochu thought it looked like a misshapen man without a head.

"Whoever would imagine a tiger trying to keep a human family safe? And a tiger that chats with birds?" Gochu's mother exclaimed. "These humans didn't hire you to stand guard and watch over them. You aren't a Hwarang![1] Next you'll be carrying a bow and arrow on your back during the day and writing poetry about the moon at night. Remember, our kind don't roam the earth with pipes like we used to!"

Gochu didn't tell his mother that there was something he learned from watching this family—something like what he learned while talking to Silla under the hibiscus tree. He didn't know what to call it, but he was just as hungry for it as he was for any meal he'd hunted.

He didn't tell her that if he could shoot a bow and arrow like the farmer, fly toward the moon and find shiny treasure like Silla, laugh like the farmer's children at dusk, or write poetry like the Hwarang, he would.

He didn't know that his mother had wondered about some of the same things as well but felt she couldn't entertain anything more than keeping Gochu and his siblings alive. The mere acknowledgment of those longings would only enrage her over their long absence from her life. The thought of Gochu being in harm's way terrified her more than anything, and she couldn't see past the fear that fogged her nocturnal eyes.

Silla often flew from tree to tree alone in the mornings, watching the mountain and the city wake up. It was her favorite time of day. Everything was beginning again, and she felt full of hope and possibility about all the good that could happen. From her vantage point of sky and trees, she could see the connectedness of the city dwellers and the mountain dwellers. She often thought, *If only I could sing in a way that would make them see it.* But Silla refused to sing, for she lacked words that could capture her heart's deep feelings.

That afternoon, Gochu told Silla about the garlic farmers farther up the mountain—how they worked and cared for the land and for one another. He told her about their bows and arrows and how the laughter he heard from their children poked at his curiosity. He wanted to know what it felt like to have laughter rise from somewhere inside of him, then break free.

Silla wanted to see what he was talking about, so they planned to meet in a thick part of the forest just beyond the house later that night.

Silla knew there were more tigers in the mountains, and she knew most of them weren't like Gochu. She thought about what made Gochu the kind of tiger he was. And she wondered, *What is it that makes me, a little bird who looks like a penguin, want to fly into the mountains to see humans who might want to shoot an arrow at me? And why would I want to spend time with a tiger who might have me for breakfast, like my eonni says Gochu should?*

Before flying to their meeting place, Silla used the pen she'd found to write a note on a large oak leaf to let her family know where she was going in case she didn't return. For the first time, she felt a little prick of worry that her trust might be her downfall.

Then she flew the pen back to the yard where she'd found it and placed it back on the wooden tree swing. She noticed a window in the house right behind the swing and saw a flutter of black and white. She was looking at herself! She watched her wings move and the way her black-and-white coloring resembled stripes when she moved—stripes like Gochu's.

Gochu was waiting for her in the shadow of a few large pine trees. It was cool and dark, and Silla found a heavenly smelling branch to perch on just above Gochu's head.

She told Gochu about returning the pen and about the reflection in the window. She exclaimed, "It was me, but when I looked closer, I also saw you!" She fluttered up from the branch to show Gochu her stripes.

Gochu laughed. "Who else would ever say we look alike when we are nothing but different?"

Silla shook her head, smiling. It was absurd, but the more time they spent together, the more she saw their similarities smack-dab alongside their stark, unmistakable differences. She wondered if she might be losing her mind or her keen eyesight.

The farmer would be out soon, so they inched closer along a path Gochu had found. Silla followed Gochu from above, flying from branch to branch.

While they waited in another hiding spot, they heard a commotion coming from the house. The commotion got louder and louder until a door flew open and all four family members ran out, shrieking.

Silla and Gochu could see the fear and desperation on their faces. Gochu stood up and sniffed the air. Smoke followed the family out of the home. Something inside had caught on fire.

As the fire spread, Gochu began pacing. The flames were now visible inside the home. He wanted to carry the family away, but he knew his presence would only add to their fear. What if they saw him and ran back to the fire-filled house?

Silla heard the children cry and noticed how it sounded like a birdsong her father used to sing to her when he was sad. She wished she could sing to them in a language they would understand, but when she opened her beak, nothing came out.

Back in the grove of trees where Silla's family lived, her sister found the oak-leaf note and read it to the rest of the family. Her mother called a meeting and gathered as many magpies as she could. They sang and shrieked to one another, and then they headed to the mountain-side together. They brought stones in their mouths to drop at anyone or anything that threatened them. As they flew closer, the smell of smoke filled their noses and the sound of rushing fire filled their ears.

Gochu couldn't watch any longer. He saw the father gathering buckets of water from the mountain stream nearby. His face was wet with sweat or tears—Gochu couldn't tell which—but all that work barely pushed the fire back at all.

Gochu noticed a large kimchi jar near the house, and he knew it was empty because he'd seen the children playing in it just days before. He ran to it and headed toward the stream, holding the jar in his mouth. The mother and children screamed when they saw him, their bodies frozen between him and their collapsing home. The little boy darted toward the side of the house to grab his bow and arrows to shoot at Gochu, but Gochu stayed on task, knowing he didn't have time to try to stop him.

Silla flew straight to the boy and pulled at the arrows in the quiver on his back, trying to keep him from hurting Gochu. Gochu filled the jar and ran back to the house, throwing water at the raging fire.

The farmer saw what was happening and stood amazed. He rubbed his eyes, and his jaw nearly touched his feet.

"The tiger is helping us!" the girl yelled.

The boy dropped his bow and stopped swatting at Silla. He looked up at her fluttering above him, with an arrow falling from her beak. "I think the magpie is helping us too," he said, eyes wide.

Silla's family and friends flew above the forest, talking to one another about the fire and wondering if Silla could still be alive. She heard them singing and squawking above the noise of the fire, and flew toward their songs.

Silla met them in the air at the top of a tall pine tree. She told them to drop their stones before they got closer and to find a way to help put the fire out. The birds called to other birds in the mountain trees, and together they filled walnut shells and anything else they could find with water and poured it over the fire. They knew if they didn't put the fire out, it would mean disaster not only for this human family but for the whole mountainside. The nuthatches, the red squirrels, and the Siberian chipmunks that lived among the pine trees all joined in.

The family of garlic farmers pinched themselves, shocked over what they were seeing. They wondered if the fire had released some kind of smoke that made their minds go mad. Whether they were dreaming or awake and witnesses to a strange magic overtaking their home and land, they joined the animals to fight the fire.

Gochu grew tired and stopped by the stream to breathe. He looked into the water as he bowed his large head for a drink. He saw bright eyes, like lights staring back at him from a big orange head. He studied the black lines and the white fur poking out beside the eyes and ears. He saw white teeth like daggers pointing at the water.

He remembered his mother saying he wasn't a Hwarang, but he felt like a poet warrior who was made to care about and fight for others, no matter how often he heard that he was made to be powerful instead of kind. He knew he needed to go on helping, no matter the cost. He stared into the water, realizing that he was staring into his own face, and he roared like he'd never roared before. He realized his soft heart made him more powerful than intimidation ever would.

The ground shook under his paws, the pine needles rattled, and the magpies joined in, imitating his roar in one song. The sound was more immense than they could hear with their ears. Together their cries paralyzed the fire. The mountain woke up and swallowed the blaze whole.

To this day, there's a lake beside the place where the farmer's new house was built. The lake is so deep and goes so far down that it reaches the place where earth and water and fire meet.

They named it Lake Jeong, and it's said that this lake can tell stories. It is known as the lake that reflects a person's face so clearly that you can see every part of their story and the face of the one who created them.

After the fire, Gochu became older, and all his orange hair began to turn white. He grew close to the family of garlic farmers, and it's been said that people who hiked up the mountain from the city would see children riding a white tiger with a bow in his mouth. The children and the tiger followed the voice of a magpie, who wore a necklace made of pine needles and hibiscus blooms, singing a song that sounded like laughter. She'd discovered how to keep beauty in the form of a song the whole forest could hear and join in.

———————◆———————

There was a little girl who lived in the city, and on days when it wasn't nice enough to swing from the wooden tree swing her dad had made her, she watched the world from the back window of her home. In the winter, she spent afternoons reading folktales about tigers that smoked pipes and about magpies and rabbits that were smart enough to rule cities like kings and queens.

She held on to a schoolbook about North America, and was particularly drawn to a page on South Dakota, a place that was far away from any of her experiences and dreams. She studied the small black-and-white pictures of hills and grassy land, of cowboys and darker-skinned people with black hair that looked like hers. There was no reason for her to feel pulled toward this book about a place so unfamiliar and far from home, but she felt the same thing Gochu and Silla felt: that there was something she could learn from studying this book and from watching the birds fly outside her window—something like what Gochu learned while talking to Silla under that hibiscus tree.

She didn't know what to call it, but she felt a longing that was bigger than anything else she desired in all the world. It was so big she often feared it would carry her farther away than the rabbit that traveled up the mountain to bring chestnuts home.

She didn't tell her mother that if she could run up into the mountain like San Toki or fly toward the moon like a magpie or roar like a tiger or write poetry like the Hwarang of the old days, defending people and goodness and mercy, she would do all of it.

One day in the spring, she went outside to sit on her swing. She saw the pen she'd lost the year before. Beside it was a leaf, like a note with scribbles on it she couldn't understand. She picked up the pen, turned over the leaf, and hiked up the mountain to record everything she saw.

She wrote about pine needle blankets and necklaces made from dried hibiscus flowers. She noticed the red squirrels and the way their fur rustled with movement and the way the nuthatches' wings stretched overhead. She found Lake Jeong and looked deep into the waters. She said hello to her reflection in the water and heard a magpie's song. She blinked and rubbed her eyes.

She stared at her image, and rather than seeing her own face, she saw the strong yet gentle face of a majestic white tiger.

———◆———

The tiger-girl became a poet and went on to fight wars with her words. She married the son of garlic farmers who lived on the mountain. Her husband was an archer who knew how to talk to animals. And their story, the one that began with the story of their parents and the animals that lived among them, birthed the stories that grew into more stories, as all stories do.

Discussion Guide

Dear friends,

I wrote this short discussion guide as a companion for you while you read *Tell Me the Dream Again* or to be used after you've read it. You can go through it alone or with another person or with a small group. Think of it as a garden gnome smiling at you while you work in the yard—a caring, non-judgmental companion. Or treat it like a walk after a big meal—a way to further digest and process the thoughts and feelings that were stirred up from the stories and reflections in the book. Feel free to work through the questions and prompts in whatever ways are most helpful, gentle, and courage-giving for you and those you love.

Grateful and shalomsick,
Tasha

CHAPTER 1: DREAMS AND TIGERS

Reflections on Chapter 1

Outside of a few words and phrases, we didn't speak Korean to one another when I was young. However, the language has always pulled at me like a map that promises to show the way home. I can pick it out on a busy city street. I know the curves and movements of its sound. I'm convinced it rests deep within me, asleep and tangled in the beating muscle fibers of my heart.

It was there in my earliest moments, pressing into my bones and ligaments, speaking straight through my mother's thoughts, mouth, and body, helping form my innermost parts. It was the language she used when she fed me and comforted me, when she was affectionate with me, and when she was most angry with me.

It was the language of her womb, my first home.

1. What stories and details passed down from your mother or father have stayed with you over time?

2. What stories and details from your family were passed on to you with missing pieces?

Something to Try

Take a few moments to write down a story, dream, memory, or cultural detail that was handed down to you. It doesn't matter if it's elaborate or simple, or whether it was intentionally passed on. Write what you remember and how you felt when you heard, lived, or recalled it. The act of writing can help us begin to unpack at a deeper level what we carry inside.

CHAPTER 2: MOTHERS AND FATHERS

Reflections on Chapter 2

Being biracial is being tied to places, people, and a history that wouldn't have welcomed me.

1. What parts of your story or personality have you tried to hush or put away in your search for belonging?

2. What people, places, and events did God use to help Tasha face the parts of herself she'd rejected as a biracial person? What people, places, and events has God used to help you face parts of yourself you've rejected?

3. What makes it hard for some people, particularly people of color, to embrace and live out their heritage and ethnic identity? Consider places, people, history, and cultural norms that intentionally or unintentionally stifle certain voices.

CHAPTER 3: SHADOWS AND FIG LEAVES

Reflections on Chapter 3

At thirteen, I instinctively knew how to sew my own fig leaves, trying to hide in plain sight.

1. Think back to times when you've felt like hiding. What parts of yourself are still in hiding?

2. What happened to Tasha when she went to Korea, expecting to find a strong sense of being home?

3. Have you ever reached for or tried to create a strong sense of home in places or things that weren't made to carry that full weight?

CHAPTER 4: SEAWEED SOUP

Reflections on Chapter 4

For thousands of years, Korean mothers have made miyeokguk for their Korean daughters when they become mothers. When I became a mother, I dumped mine down the drain.

1. What foods remind you of the nourishing love of a parent, grandparent, or other family member?

2. What foods have you turned away from, whether for health reasons, dieting reasons, or because they made you feel like you didn't fit in?

3. Food is a love language. As you think back on your life story, consider it in terms of food—the way you were fed and nourished. Write down the tastes, scents, and people involved. Which of those colors, spices, and flavors are part of your dinner table today?

Something to Try

Make something that nourished you with love when you were growing up. As you gather ingredients at the store or from your kitchen, thank God for these tangible, tasteable things, and let yourself remember how they were given to you. Research the origins of that dish, and write down one thing you learn. Invite someone into the making and eating of this food, such as a child, a spouse, a friend, or the person who first fed it to you.

CHAPTER 5: STRANGERS AND SCARS

Reflections on Chapter 5

I was six when I found out my sister and I didn't have the same father. I was six when I realized that someone could be married more than once. I was six when I started asking a lot of questions about how families are made and how they fall apart.

> 1. It's easy to see how our fragmented and broken family histories hinder us. In what ways can they also inform us, deepen our empathy, and strengthen our ability to care for ourselves and others?

Moses' story is full of familial fracture, loss, loneliness, wandering, brokenness, and dual-cultured struggles, but also a God who pursed him—not after all these colliding details were resolved, but right in the middle of them. His ancestors, his cultural identity, his faith, and his own relationship with God are woven together with the making of his own family and the generations to come.

> 2. Think about the years of pain, anger, and grief that Moses lived through and how God met him and guided him through those parts of his story. How did Moses' dual identity as the son of a Hebrew mother and an adoptive Egyptian mother shape him as a leader, a husband, and a father?

CHAPTER 6: SHALOMSICK

Reflections on Chapter 6

The first time I read the story of the woman who broke open her jar of perfume at Jesus' feet, as well as the story of the woman at the well and the story of the bleeding woman, it was my mother's face, my mother's tears, my mother's desperation, my mother's humility that I pictured.

1. How did God pursue Tasha when she was a child? How did she begin to understand her desperation for Jesus?

2. How has God met you in the margins of what's expected and acceptable?

CHAPTER 7: REMEMBRANCE AND HEALING

Reflections on Chapter 7

These days when I feel lonely in my Asian American body or when the world feels too harsh and violent toward Asian American bodies, I intentionally go back to my memories. I remember the moments when I felt most at home.

1. As you look back over your life, when do you remember feeling most at home? Describe these moments in a journal or talk about them with a friend.

2. What pains or barriers have you experienced in seeking a place to belong?

3. How do you practice remembering what God has done in your life and in your family's history?

CHAPTER 8: HAN AND HOPE

Reflections on Chapter 8

Sharing our stories brings other people's stories into the light. Maybe you need to share your story with a big crowd, or maybe with just one other person. Maybe you will sing or scribble down poetry or raise your voice for justice in a way that challenges and creates opportunities for change. Maybe the sharing of your story will cause a jolting, uncomfortable response, or maybe the impact will be quiet and slow, an almost invisible awakening at work. No matter what it looks like, every story shared in love is an act of courage and kindness that will connect people and multiply good.

1. Are there stories that stay hidden inside you? Why do you think it's difficult to let certain stories out?

2. Picture the kind of community that would make you feel safe enough to share your stories. Have you ever had a place like that? Do you have a place like that now?

Something to Try

Write a prayer, asking God for a safe space to share your story and your whole self.

CHAPTER 9: GHOSTS AND GLORY

Reflections on Chapter 9

Am I bad because I'm biracial? And if so, which side of me is the ugly side? Which part of my ethnic heritage represents Patji, and which one represents Kongji?

1. What narratives have guided your decisions about what is good or bad, better or best—both in the world and within yourself?

There's movement toward the Kingdom of God in places we'd never expect, and it begins with stories in desert places and cemeteries, stories about nightmares and ghosts. God is not afraid of the one who is thirsty, the one who runs away, the foreigner, the betrayed, the lonely, the battered, and the fearful.

God's love stories start with people like these.

1. Where would you never expect a love story of God to begin? (Be honest!)

Something to Try

Set aside a few minutes every morning or night (or whenever works best for you), and pray these breath prayers:

Breathe in: *God, you are not afraid of anyone.*
Breathe out: *Show me how you love the ones I'd least expect to be loved.*
Breathe in: *God, you are not afraid of my ghosts.*
Breathe out: *I am loved in every part. I am whole.*

CHAPTER 10: JESUS AND JEONG

Reflections on Chapter 10

I couldn't embrace the good news of the gospel or the hope of Jesus' Kingdom come, here and now, until I embraced the good news written in my thick mixed hair, the face of Jesus' Kingdom staring back at me in the mirror. I had to learn not only that he didn't mind my kimchi-breath prayers but that if he were here with me in the flesh, he would have kimchi breath too.

1. What parts within you feel rejected?

2. Can you imagine Jesus with you in those places and particularities?

Glossary

AIGOO: a phrase used to express a variety of emotions, including disbelief, disappointment, shock, or surprise

BANCHAN: a collective name for Korean side dishes

CHUSEOK: Korean harvest festival

DORAEMON: Japanese manga cartoon series about a robotic cat

GAMSAHAMNIDA: thank you

GOCHUGARU: Korean chili powder

HALMONI: grandmother

HARABOJI: grandfather

HORANGI: tiger

HWANGAP: traditional Korean sixtieth birthday celebration

IMO: maternal aunt

INJEOLMI: type of sweet rice cake

KONGNAMUL: soybean sprouts

MANDU: Korean dumplings

MEOGGO: to eat

MIYEOKGUK: seaweed soup

MUGUK: radish soup

MUL: water

NAENGMYEON: cold noodle dish made from flour and starch originating in North Korea

PAJEON: Korean pancake with scallions

SONGPYEON: half-moon shaped rice cake

SOONDUBU JJIGAE: tofu stew

SUJEBI: traditional Korean soup made with hand-torn dough flakes

TTEOKGUK: Korean rice cake soup

Acknowledgments

In some ways, writing these acknowledgments feels more challenging than writing a book chapter. There are so many people who were part of this book and the stories shared in it, and if I tried to record everyone, I'd have a second book. Being connected to you, dear reader, whether you're someone I've never met, someone I know online, someone I knew for a brief but important time, or someone I've known my whole life, fills me with overwhelming gratitude.

To Matt: In the beginning of "us," you remembered that I like to look in windows and create stories from them, and you've been the one, more than any other, to remind me to be true to my own story ever since. Thank you for being the biggest part of my moving from rejection to embrace and healing—and for not only encouraging me, but joining me for the journey. Thank you for everything you've taken on and let go of so I could write this book. You are the most faithful and steadfast person I know, and everyone around you is impacted for good because of it, especially me. If this book never happened, you would still be there and we would still be us. You are my favorite, my best friend, and I love you and our life together.

To Asher, Timo, and Everly: You are the cotton-candy sunsets that take my breath away, the golden light bursting from the morning-sun hope of a new day, and the gentle moonlight. Being your 엄마 is the greatest gift and best adventure of my life, and it always will be. Parts of this book were written while doing e-learning during a pandemic, and other parts were written later, while waiting in your school pickup lines, during bass lessons, tennis and track practice, or garden club meetings, or with video games and your laughter (and fighting) in the background. Without knowing it, you've consistently reminded me of what's important, true, good, and beautiful, and that guided me as I wrote. I hope the words and stories on these pages might help you embrace your own unique and connected stories someday, along with the perfectly beloved image bearer you are.

To my parents, Jim and Jeong: You fed me lessons that the places where worlds collide—places of nuance, tension, diversity, curiosity, not knowing, forgiveness, and compassion—are beautiful and necessary. You are the ones who first taught me to be curious, to value my own story and stories different from mine, and to try to see the world, listen to it, and learn from it in any way I could. I'm so glad your combined story is the place where God chose for mine to begin. I'm so proud to be your daughter. Thank you for everything.

To Cathy: I treasure the stories that only you and I share, and I love the new stories of "us" that are just now being written. Our sister stories remind me that family ties can bloom late, travel at their own pace, and still become something beautiful. Thank you for teaching me to "make a nose," for being my eonni, and for always bringing laughter and wasabi deviled eggs.

To my mother- and father-in-law (in-love), who love big and love quietly, and have cheered me on throughout: I'm blessed to call you family. Thank you.

To those who told me I could write and should write, and who urged me to write more and to keep writing: Mr. Richards in high school English; Tony Ardizzone, who challenged me in the ways I needed most and made me believe I could write, and write from the heart; and Corinne Gunter, who invited me to Rwanda to tell stories; thank you for handing me a pen and calling me out from hiding.

To Sandy Dragon: Thank you for supporting me with such belief, steadfastness, and truth-telling, for talking me down from a whole lot of ledges while writing, and for the endless hours you spent reading my words before anyone else did—as if you didn't have a thousand things on your plate already. You have stuck by my side as few else have. Your faithfulness and generosity have held me.

To Tanorria Askew Nickson: Thank you for being my friend, and for shared meals, unwavering support, checking in, and your unapologetic embrace of dreaming big. Thank you for sharing your dreams and for dreaming with me when I shared mine.

To all the women of the Indy Asian American Sisterhood, especially Tara VanderWoude, Soo James, Rachel Cho, Ann Derksen, Erica O'Neil, and Angel Ho, whose friendship and shared hope and han mean so much to me. Thank you for being such a big part of this book and for the safe space you are.

To our small group and dear friends: Natalie and Keith Back, Kim and Eugene Park, and Justin and Linnea Baxtron. Thank you for your care, consistency, and support. I can't imagine our family without all of yours.

To Leslie Hughes and Lisa Duhamell, the best neighbor-friends I've ever had: Thank you for being such safe places while I was first writing this book. I miss living next door to both of you.

To my Grace Fishers church family: Thank you for caring for our family throughout this time and much more.

To Alia Joy: Thank you for inspiring me with your own writing and for inviting me into friendship when you barely knew me. Thank you for believing in my words and championing me when you didn't have to. It feels as though we've known each other much longer than we have—maybe in another universe overflowing with new mercies. I would have given up a long time ago if it weren't for you.

To Grace P. Cho: Your warmth, welcome, and wisdom have impacted my writing from the time when I knew you only as "Grace, the writer I wish I knew," until you became "Grace, the writer, editor, and my friend." Thank you for being a safe Korean sister who fed me in more ways than you know, from late-night ramen to poetry to word care to always believing in the stories I had to tell and to telling me the truth. Thank you for affirming my Koreanness and for always saving a spot for me.

To Michelle Reyes and Dorina Lazo Gilmore-Young: You are the writer-friends who have shared your worlds with me and welcomed all of mine. Thank you for friendship, your faithfulness, your cheering-for, and so much more. Thank you for always believing in this book and in me. Writing and life are so much better with each of you.

To these groups that have pulled up a seat for me and supported me in this book journey—my writers' group, the Korean American Sisterhood of Writers, #tamalesdimsum kimchi, and #kimchisisterhood: Thank you for sharing your lives and your creative work with me (Sarah Westfall, Sara Billups, Jenai Auman, Kyunghee Kim, Natasha Akery, Maggie Johnson, Kathy Khang, and others mentioned elsewhere).

To my (in)courage sisters: I learn from each of you regularly, and each of you has been part of the journey of this book. I feel so honored to be with, among, and alongside you. Thank you for being a wide, welcoming space.

To the women of Redbud Writers Guild: Thank you for your support and encouragement.

To my agent, Jevon Bolden, who believed in me and these stories from the start—I'll never forget our first conversation. Thank you for championing me.

To the Momentum team at Tyndale, and especially Jillian Schlossberg, who was safe and visionary from the beginning and throughout everything (thank you for taking a chance on me); my smart and tender editor, Stephanie Rische; and Sarah Atkinson, who asked the best and most honest questions. Thank you all for making this book experience better than I could have dreamed of.

Last, and most important, to Jesus: You are the one who has pursued all of me without ceasing from my mother's womb, who has always been with me, who will never leave me, who I now know would eat kimchi with me, and who has never stopped loving me and leading me in love and toward love. You are everything, and I am yours. Thank you for being Immanuel.

Notes

CHAPTER 2: MOTHERS AND FATHERS
1. See John 17.
2. See John 1:1.

CHAPTER 3: SHADOWS AND FIG LEAVES
1. See Genesis 3:7.
2. See Psalm 139:14, NIV.
3. Strong's Hebrew Concordance, s.v. "meod," https://bibleapps.com /strongs/hebrew/3966.htm.
4. See Genesis 3:9.
5. See Genesis 4:9, 16:8.

CHAPTER 4: SEAWEED SOUP
1. See Psalm 34:8.

CHAPTER 5: STRANGERS AND SCARS
1. See Exodus 1:15–2:10.

CHAPTER 6: SHALOMSICK
1. See Mark 14:1-9; John 4:1-42; Matthew 9:20-22.
2. Elizabeth Rosner, *Survivor Café: The Legacy of Trauma and the Labyrinth of Memory* (Berkeley: Counterpoint Press, 2017), 17, 43.
3. Andrew Sung Park, *The Wounded Heart of God: The Asian Concept of Han and the Christian Doctrine of Sin* (Nashville: Abingdon Press, 1993), 41.

4. Joanna Ho, *Eyes That Kiss in the Corners* (New York: HarperCollins, 2021).

5. See Matthew 18:20.

CHAPTER 7: REMEMBRANCE AND HEALING

1. Elizabeth Rosner, *Survivor Café: The Legacy of Trauma and the Labyrinth of Memory* (Berkeley: Counterpoint Press, 2017), 19.

2. See Matthew 26:17-29; Luke 22:19; John 13:1-17.

3. See 1 Corinthians 9:23, NIV.

4. Official Report of the Nineteenth Annual Conference of Charities and Correction (1892), 46–59. Reprinted in Richard H. Pratt, "The Advantages of Mingling Indians with Whites," *Americanizing the American Indians: Writings by the "Friends of the Indian" 1880–1900* (Cambridge, MA: Harvard University Press, 1973), 260–271.

CHAPTER 8: HAN AND HOPE

1. See Ephesians 3:18.

2. "The Secret of a Tiger's Roar," American Institute of Physics— Inside Science News Service, December 29, 2000, https://www.sciencedaily.com/releases/2000/12/001201152406.htm.

3. "Secret of a Tiger's Roar."

CHAPTER 9: GHOSTS AND GLORY

1. *Asian Americans*, produced by S. Leo Chiang, Geeta Gandbhir, Grace Lee, and Renee Tajima-Peña, aired May 2020, on PBS.

2. See Genesis 16:13.

CHAPTER 10: JESUS AND JEONG

1. See Matthew 1:2-16; Luke 3:23-38.

EPILOGUE: SILLA AND GOCHU: A FOLKTALE

1. Hwarang, sometimes called Flowering Knights, were a group of young, highly trained warriors in ancient Korea from the sixth century to the tenth century AD.